THE NARCISSISTIC ABUSE RECOVERY BLUEPRINT

A REVOLUTIONARY APPROACH THAT MERGES REAL-LIFE EXPERIENCE WITH GROUNDBREAKING SCIENCE

K. C. MALLETTE

CONTENTS

PREFACE

As I embark on this exploration of the intricate landscape of narcissistic abuse recovery, it is with a deep sense of commitment and empathy for those who have navigated the complex journey from victimhood to empowerment. With over three decades of personal experience in psychology and narcissistic abuse recovery, coupled with a genuine desire to shed light on the shadows of emotional abuse, I present *"The Narcissistic Abuse Recovery Blueprint."*

In this comprehensive guide, we delve into the labyrinth of narcissistic abuse, unraveling its layers to provide a profound understanding of its impact on victims. From the psychological intricacies that make individuals susceptible targets to the lasting effects that echo through their lives, each chapter is a step toward illumination and healing.

The chapters are strategically designed to serve as a roadmap for recovery, combining the latest insights from the science of healing with practical strategies for rebuilding one's life. From dissecting the anatomy of a target to the crucial role of boundaries, self-worth, and community support, each section addresses a vital aspect of the recovery process.

This book is not merely a compilation of clinical observations; it is a heartfelt guide that speaks directly to you, the reader, acknowledging the pain, confusion, and challenges you may be facing. It is an offering of support, validation, and practical tools to navigate the path toward renewal and self-discovery.

In a world where the prevalence of narcissistic abuse extends across genders, ages, and backgrounds, this guide seeks to reach those who may not even be aware they are trapped in such relationships. It emphasizes the importance of empathy, self-care, and understanding the unique nature of each survivor's journey.

As we embark on this expedition together, my aim is to empower you with knowledge, inspire you with narratives of resilience, and guide you toward a future marked by healing and hope. The journey of recovery is inherently personal, but with the right tools and understanding, you can emerge not just as a survivor but as someone who embraces a new self—a self defined by strength, authenticity, and the unwavering ability to thrive beyond the shadows of narcissistic abuse.

K. C. Mallette

INTRODUCTION

Amelia stood at the crossroads of despair on a quiet December night in Texas. She felt trapped in a suffocating relationship, lost and hopeless. The weight of a narcissistic partner's manipulative words and actions bore down on her, shrouding her in darkness. She questioned her worth and reality due to emotional abuse from her narcissistic husband. The isolation, the gaslighting, and the erosion of her self-esteem seemed insurmountable.

But here's the twist—Amelia finally broke free. In the midst of that cold December night, she discovered the strength within herself to escape the clutches of narcissistic abuse. Now, imagine for a moment that Amelia is not just a character in a story. She is a representation of countless individuals trapped in similar cycles of emotional torment. And the good news? Amelia's escape is not an isolated victory.

If you or someone you care about is ensnared in the web of narcissistic abuse, know this: liberation is possible. Amelia found her way out, and so can you or your loved one.

Now, let's delve into the insidious nature of narcissistic abuse—the very labyrinth Amelia navigated. Imagine a narcissistic manipulator employing projection and reality-bending tactics to maintain control. Take, for instance, the art of projecting blame. They skillfully blame others for their own faults, accusing their victims of the same behaviors. This leaves individuals bewildered, questioning their own actions and reality.

Gaslighting, another insidious technique, involves manipulating someone into doubting their perception of reality. Narcissists may deny saying or doing something, making victims question their sanity. But it doesn't end there. The narcissist has many tools, like silent treatment and false empathy, to manipulate others. They also use love-bombing and devaluation. Each method serves to maintain a toxic cycle of abuse, perpetuating dependence and confusion.

Victims need to know these sneaky tactics to escape narcissistic abuse. Imagine meeting someone who seems charming but actually has a secret plan. According to Psychology Today, this initial meeting often feels like entering a web where the spider is both creator and captor. The narcissist's charm becomes a snare, pulling you into a dynamic that, at first, may seem exhilarating.

Yet, as you delve deeper, the cracks start to show. Their need for admiration becomes insatiable, and their empathy becomes superficial. Your achievements might be met with subtle jealousy, a foreshadowing of the emotional storm to come. The manipulations and gaslighting start early, like seeds planted in your trust.

As the relationship progresses, so does the emotional toll. Anxiety creeps in as you navigate the unpredictable terrain of their moods. You find yourself questioning your worth and your reality, bending to fit their narrative. The narcissist gradually isolates you from friends and family to maintain control.

So, if you've ever felt the weight of confusion and self-doubt after encountering someone who seemed too good to be true, you're not alone. This journey through the labyrinth of narcissistic encounters is a shared experience. Imagine a life where the shadows of narcissistic abuse no longer cast a pall over your well-being. The desire for peace, self-worth, and empowerment in relationships flickers in the hearts of those who have weathered the storm of emotional manipulation. This book is your compass, guiding you toward a brighter existence.

Imagine a future where you escape narcissistic abuse and thrive with strength. In the pages that follow, you'll learn about the intricacies of narcissistic abuse and how to recover and become empowered. Together, we'll embark on a journey to heal, understand, and reclaim the light, even in the darkest nights of December.

I've learned about narcissistic abuse by experiencing it firsthand in my own family. Having weathered the storm myself, I've stood shoulder to shoulder with individuals facing narcissistic abuse, navigating the tumultuous seas of emotional manipulation. This book is more than just words on paper. It's a lifeline that comes from my journey and the experiences of others who found healing and empowerment.

I know the pain, confusion, and isolation that accompany these experiences. Yet, I also know the resilience within each person to reclaim their narrative and rebuild their lives. This book isn't about offering generic advice. It's about sharing proven strategies, scientifically-backed insights, and personal experiences that resonate with the intricate dance of narcissistic abuse.

So, let's journey together from the shadows into the light. This book will help you reclaim your life, rebuild your self-worth, and forge real connections.

In Chapter 1, "The Narcissistic Labyrinth," we'll explore narcissistic abuse. We'll untangle the threads that bind you, bringing clarity and understanding. This will set the stage for your journey from victim to survivor, and then survivor to thriver.

CHAPTER 1
THE NARCISSISTIC LABYRINTH

Narcissists are like parasitic bugs that leech onto you and essentially suck the life out of you, then when you are no longer useful, they discard you.

SILVI SAXENA

In the labyrinth of human emotions, where shadows dance with the light, lies a complex realm known to many as the "Narcissistic Labyrinth." Picture yourself caught in a complex web of relationships where reality and illusion blend together, and the emotional landscape is tricky and captivating. As you step into this enigmatic world, picture encounters with individuals who, like parasites, latch onto your vulnerabilities, draining the life force from your very soul. Silvi Saxena describes narcissists as bugs that drain your essence until they discard you.

Handling a relationship with a narcissist is a delicate dance.

Their quest for control can lead to manipulation and emotional exploitation, damaging self-esteem. To maintain a sense of self, it's important to set boundaries and recognize your emotions. For instance, when dealing with a narcissistic boss or understanding narcissism in relationships, you can use strategies to manage expectations, draw boundaries, and avoid futile arguments. In this chapter, you will learn about the underlying concepts of narcissism, including different behaviors and manipulative tactics. It also covers the ups and downs of narcissistic relationships.

UNDERSTANDING THE SPECTRUM OF NARCISSISM

Decoding narcissism is like solving a puzzle with pieces of self-absorption and entitlement. On the vast spectrum of narcissism, we all start out self-centered, but we can grow and become more aware and empathetic. The Narcissistic Personality Inventory (NPI) measures this trait, showcasing that most fall within the average range. However, the line between healthy self-love and pathological narcissism is thin, determining the nature of our relationships.

Navigating this spectrum is vital to distinguishing between healthy self-love and toxic manifestations. It's not merely about self-esteem but a profound hunger for attention and a belief in one's unique, deserving status (Simon, 2018). Distinguishing between common narcissism and pathological narcissistic personality disorder (NPD) is crucial. Narcissistic traits are common, but NPD, which affects only 1% of people, impairs daily life and relationships due to a lack of empathy.

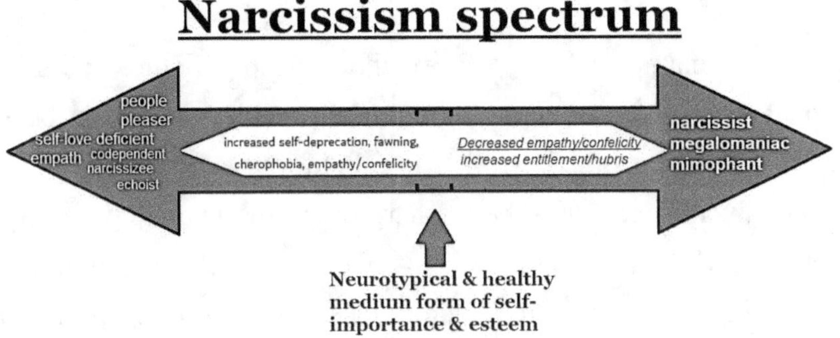

Figure 1. Illustration of narcissism spectrum (Source: Wikimedia, Creative Commons)

TYPES OF NARCISSISM

Understanding different types of narcissism is crucial for coping. It helps you recognize manipulative behaviors, set boundaries, and safeguard your well-being. Identifying narcissistic traits in relationships empowers you to navigate these dynamics effectively. By recognizing the small differences, you can avoid manipulation and have better relationships. Remember, knowledge is your protection against narcissism. It helps you regain control and maintain your emotional well-being.

Overt Narcissist

Imagine a person exuding an air of superiority, craving the spotlight, and dismissing the feelings of others. This is an overt narcissist who feels entitled, seeks attention, and belittles others. They often show off their achievements, lack empathy, and use people for their own benefit. Recognizing these signs is your first line of defense (Chughtai, 2023).

Concrete examples help solidify the concept. Picture an individual constantly bragging about their achievements, a boss taking credit for others' work while belittling subordinates, or a friend always needing to be in charge. These scenarios provide a snapshot of overt narcissist behavior in action. Recognizing and navigating the overt narcissistic landscape is a crucial skill. To protect yourself from an overt narcissist, learn their behavior, understand what causes it, and use coping strategies.

Covert Narcissist

When we hear "narcissist," we often conjure images of loud, assertive individuals basking in self-importance. But there's a stealthier version lurking in the shadows: the covert narcissist. This introverted breed conceals their insecurities beneath a veil of self-importance, making them a subtle yet formidable force (Raypole, 2023).

Picture the overt narcissist as the room's loudest presence, while the covert counterpart is the master of disguise. Covert narcissists fly under the radar, and their subtle manipulation often escapes notice for extended periods. While both share insecurities, the difference lies in expression; covert narcissists internalize their self-importance, focusing intensely on their need for attention.

"Covert narcissists are people who fly under the radar. Even if you've been in a relationship with someone for years, their covert narcissism may be so subtle that you're not even aware of it for a very long time," explains psychologist Dr. Susan Albers.

Communal Narcissist

Have you ever met someone who seemingly radiates altruism but leaves you questioning their true intentions? You might have just encountered a communal narcissist (Arzt, 2021). Communal narcissists set themselves apart from the classic narcissistic archetype. Instead of showing off, they camouflage their grandiosity under the guise of extreme helpfulness. Imagine someone who claims, "I am an amazing listener," or boasts about being the "best parent on this planet." These self-proclamations of communal virtues are the communal narcissist's modus operandi.

While communal narcissists may not intentionally deceive, their charismatic self-proclamations protect them against their own doubts. Recognize that they might be caught in a web of self-deception rather than intentional deceit. Their need to believe in their exceptionalism could be a subconscious plea for validation.

Antagonistic Narcissist

The need to connect and attach is a strong force that binds us together in relationships. However, there is a stark contrast within this rich fabric—the world of antagonistic narcissists. They thrive on a twisted dynamic of predation, competition, and parasitism.

In the realm of antagonistic attachment, narcissists view relationships as power struggles. Instead of collaboration, they seek domination (Hart et al., 2022). Their toolkit includes overt acts of aggression like berating, name-calling, and physical intimidation. But it also uses sneakier tactics like ignoring, insulting, and threatening indirectly. The objective is to emotionally and physically oppress others, ensuring a perpetual sense of control.

Antagonistic narcissists have a big difference between how they act in public and in private. This is similar to covert narcissism and makes things confusing and dangerous. By unraveling the layers of deception, we empower ourselves to protect against the unseen predator and break the cycle of trauma that can permeate our relationships and communities.

Malignant Narcissists

In the intricate dance of human relationships, some individuals operate on a different wavelength—an ominous frequency that resonates with entitlement and self-centered motives. This is the realm of malignant narcissists, a breed of individuals for whom the world orbits around the unwavering belief that "It's all about me."

Malignant narcissists are not just run-of-the-mill, self-centered personalities (Raypole, 2019). At the very top of the self-centered scale, they have a sense of entitlement to everything they do. These people exhibit an unyielding need for control, a severe lack of empathy, and an alternate reality where their viewpoints are supreme.

To protect yourself from a malignant narcissist, you must understand their twisted psyche. By embracing these insights and adopting a strategic approach, you can navigate the stormy seas of a relationship with a malignant narcissist and emerge with your well-being intact.

NARCISSISM IN POPULAR CULTURE VS. REALITY

In the captivating world of pop culture, narcissism takes center stage. It showcases a range of characters, from charmingly self-absorbed to outright megalomaniacal. Characters such as Jay Gatsby and Patrick Bateman have become famous for their narcissism. They represent societal fascination and the nuances of the human psyche. Yet, real-life manifestations often defy these glamorous or malevolent stereotypes (Remes, 2023).

Narcissism has its roots in ancient mythology, where Narcissus himself played a part. Today, it continues to influence the rise of influencers and social media personas. Navigating this cultural landscape requires deciphering between the captivating narratives spun for entertainment and the more subtle, complex expressions of narcissism permeating our daily interactions. In a world where reality and fiction continually blur, a nuanced understanding becomes crucial.

Empirical Insights: Sociocultural Impact Explored

When we look at real-life examples, we can see how history, culture, age, and technology affect narcissism. A survey of 1,025 individuals from both West and East Germany revealed strong connections between background and narcissistic traits. The study showed how individualism, collectivism, and a fulfilling life are all intertwined. Let's explore key factors influencing the sociocultural impact of narcissism:

1. **Narcissism Epidemic:** The use of tools like the Narcissistic Personality Inventory (NPI) has shown an increase in narcissism. This increase is especially notable in modern Western societies, like the United States (Vater et al., 2018).
2. **Cultural Influence:** Cultural factors greatly influence narcissistic traits. Individualistic settings, like the United States, have higher narcissism scores than collectivistic cultures, such as China.
3. **Age Group:** Age plays a role, with narcissism generally decreasing over time. The above-mentioned German reunification study also underscores age-related differences.
4. **Technological Developments:** Studies report that increasing technological advancements contribute to the "empty self." This results in fostering an environment conducive to narcissistic expressions.

Cultural Trends and Narcissism

In today's selfie-driven culture, social media subtly nurtures narcissistic tendencies. While excessive posting isn't the direct cause of narcissism, the constant comparison for attention on these platforms affects self-esteem, fostering competitive acquaintanceships over deep friendships.

Understanding the dimensions of narcissism becomes a guiding light in navigating the complex interplay between cultural trends and relationships. From the allure of social media to relationship intricacies, recognizing the dance between validation, self-worth, and genuine connection is essential.

1. **Social Media and Narcissism:** Researchers identify links between narcissism and social media, noting that high grandiosity leads to downward social comparison, while vulnerability results in upward social comparison. Higher grandiosity and entitlement correlate with more frequent posts, and vulnerability introduces a nuanced emotional dimension (Dong et al., 2023).

2. **Authenticity Amid Trends:** Recognizing the impact of a partner's narcissistic traits on mental health is crucial in the era of social media. Balancing relationship needs with self-care involves introspection, compassion, and authenticity, emphasizing that genuine self-worth doesn't hinge on excessive adoration.

Narcissism in Popular Culture

As we navigate the fascinating interplay between historical figures and contemporary celebrities, the tapestry of narcissism in popular culture continues to unfold. From conquests to concert stages, the allure and challenges of those driven by an insatiable need for self-validation take the spotlight!

Ever wondered what it takes to be at the top of your game? Well, it's a wild ride where self-confidence can sometimes spill over into full-blown narcissism. Let's dive into the juicy details of some famous narcissists, both from the pages of history and the glitzy stages of today.

1. **Alexander the Great:** Imagine Alexander, not just a conqueror but a narcissistic showstopper, orchestrating a spectacle for personal glory. Whether ally or adversary, his grandiose visions took center stage—a true narcissistic conqueror!

2. **Henry VIII:** Henry VIII, with charisma to spare, reveals a dark side of egotism through multiple wives, beheadings, and an obsessive pursuit of a male heir. His lack of empathy and focus on appearance paint a vivid picture of a ruler entwined with vanity.

3. **Napoleon Bonaparte:** Ever heard of the "Napoleon Complex?" Napoleon aggressively compensated for his lack of height by seeking power. His journey from fantasy to reality is a narcissistic tale etched in history.

4. **Disney's *Tangled*:** Even in animated worlds, narcissism weaves its intricate threads. In *Tangled*, Mother Gothel

embodies a narcissistic parent, manipulating and controlling with self-absorbed intensity—a reminder that narcissism transcends reality.

NARCISSISTIC BEHAVIORS AND TACTICS

Ever find yourself caught in the crossfire of someone's narcissistic maneuvers? Imagine the *Bait and Switch*—a classic move where narcissists, charming at first, gradually morph into manipulative beings, leaving you bewildered. Take love bombing, a tactic where compliments and affection shower down like confetti until you're ensnared, only for the narcissist to reveal their true colors. Social media, a playground for narcissistic behaviors, showcases the "Narcissistic Feed" dance. Whether it's posting relentlessly, seeking likes, or comparing and excluding, these tactics reveal the intricate web narcissists weave in their pursuit of adoration.

Gaslighting and Manipulation

Gaslighting, a sinister form of emotional abuse, plays out like a psychological chess match, leaving you questioning your own reality. Psychologist Dr. Chivonna Childs unravels this mental manipulation where the aggressor skillfully distorts events, making you doubt your own experiences. Originating from the 1938 play *Gas Light*, this tactic aims to undermine your confidence, leaving you grappling with self-doubt (Sweet, 2023).

Spotting gaslighting involves recognizing cues like one-sided validation, disguised insensitivity, and a refusal to let you express yourself. In a gaslighting scenario, your concerns may be manipulated, leaving you questioning your perception. Dr. Childs advises a delicate response, including early confrontation, seeking support, and prioritizing mental health, to break free from this toxic cycle and foster growth in relationships.

Narcissistic Love Bombing Cycle

Embarking on the intricate journey of interpersonal relationships, you may encounter the phenomenon known as the narcissistic love bombing cycle (Drescher, 2023). This term encapsulates a manipulative pattern often displayed by individuals with narcissistic traits, particularly in the initial stages of a connection.

Understanding the narcissistic love bombing cycle is pivotal for recognizing and navigating manipulative dynamics within your relationships. By identifying warning signs and fostering self-awareness, you can navigate these intricate patterns with a focus on maintaining your emotional well-being and making informed decisions about the trajectory of your relationship.

Narcissistic Discard

Ever been in a relationship where things took a sudden, confusing turn, leaving you feeling lost and abandoned? If you've tangled with someone showing signs of narcissistic personality disorder (NPD), you might be familiar with the rollercoaster ride of the discard phase (Burgemeester, 2023). Not all narcissists follow the same script when it comes to discarding someone. It's like dealing with a wildcard; they might blame you for everything or cut ties without a second thought. Brace yourself during this stage, as things tend to get even more abusive and manipulative. Your goal is to maintain control even as they make their exit.

During the discard phase, understand the self-centered motivations behind the discard, peeling back layers to reveal their complex nature. Coping after the discard phase involves your resilience, self-care, and establishing firm boundaries, emphasizing that it's not a reflection of your worth. Empower yourself by recognizing patterns, focusing on your well-being, and using tools like therapy for recovery.

THE NARCISSISTIC RELATIONSHIP CYCLE

In the intricate dance of narcissistic relationships, the cycle unfolds with a sinister elegance. Picture the grand overture of love bombing, where narcissists shower their prey with affection and grand gestures, creating an illusionary world of bliss. Here, compliments flow like a river, and promises of an eternal connection sound like sweet poetry. Yet, the enchantment is fleeting as the stage shifts to devaluation, a dark act where criticisms rain down and affection dwindles like a dying ember. The partner, once placed on a pedestal, now grapples with emotional isolation. Then comes the grand finale: the discard, or, in some instances, the hypnotic hoovering, a desperate attempt to pull the partner back into the toxic waltz.

Figure 2. Illustration of a narcissistic abuse cycle (Source: Narcissistic Abuse Rehab, Creative Commons)

Unveiling this cycle is like deciphering a psychological thriller, with each phase laden with manipulative tactics and emotional turbulence. As someone with practical knowledge of narcissistic abuse, my mission is to guide you through the shadows, offer insights that empower you, and unravel the intricate web of the narcissistic relationship cycle (Schneider, 2015).

The Highs and Lows

Embarking on a narcissistic relationship rollercoaster is like riding waves of euphoria and crashing into valleys of despair. In the initial stages, the narcissist showers you with love and adoration, creating a fairy-tale atmosphere that seems too good to be true. These highs are intoxicating, with a magnetic force drawing you closer. However, the tide turns swiftly. The adoration morphs into manipulation, and the once-charming partner becomes a master at emotional turbulence. The lows are marked by gaslighting, blame-shifting, and a constant erosion of self-worth, leaving you in the shadows of doubt.

The Reasons Behind the Cycle

Understanding the intricacies of the narcissistic relationship cycle reveals a power play rooted in the narcissist's deep-seated insecurities. The initial love-bombing phase serves a strategic purpose—it establishes control by creating emotional dependency. As the cycle progresses, the narcissist's need for validation takes a darker turn, leading to devaluation and emotional abuse. The fluctuation between idealization and devaluation maintains a toxic equilibrium, fueling the narcissist's insatiable ego while keeping you tethered to the tumultuous ride.

Recognizing the Signs and Breaking Free

Spotting the signs within this turbulent relationship cycle is crucial for reclaiming your emotional well-being. Gaslighting, constant criticism, and an inability to empathize are red flags. Breaking free requires courage and a strategic plan. Reach out to a support network, be it friends, family, or professionals. Set firm boundaries, prioritize self-care, and seek therapy to untangle the emotional knots. Recognizing that the highs are manipulative tools and the lows are detrimental to your mental health becomes the compass guiding you toward liberation. Remember, the path to freedom starts with understanding the cycle and finding the strength to step off the narcissistic rollercoaster.

THE NARCISSIST RED FLAGS CHECKLIST: A GUIDE TO PROTECT YOUR EMOTIONAL WELL-BEING

While navigating the dense forest of relationships, it's not always easy to spot the lurking snakes. Ignoring red flags out of love or ignorance often leads to a perilous entanglement with a narcissist. As survivors yearn for a time machine to identify these red flags earlier, this non-exhaustive checklist emerges as a beacon of awareness (Pedersen, 2022). Recognizing these signs isn't a journey into the past but a guide for the present and a shield for the future.

The Look of Narc's Friends on You

When the narcissist's friends enter your life, pay attention. Their eyes may tell tales of your partner's past. Pitying glances may reveal knowledge, and subtle doubts could linger—a silent warning that you're stepping into a complex world. Pay attention to a friend's quizzical look, which might be a silent commentary on what they know about the narcissist's history.

Have Very Low to Zero Friends

Different narcissists often have similar patterns. Narcissists lack genuine connections and keep their abusive traits hidden with minimal social circles. They may claim to have friends, but you'll rarely interact with them. Your attempts to engage with a narcissist's friends are often met with resistance or excuses.

Doesn't Like Your Friends

Narcissists fear external support. They manipulate you, projecting your friends as toxic and coaxing you into isolation. Recognizing this red flag involves understanding their control over your social circle. Your partner consistently refuses to interact with your friends, portraying them as a threat to the relationship.

Double Standards for Friends of the Opposite Sex

Narcissists excel at emotional manipulation, intentionally introducing the opposite sex to incite jealousy. Meanwhile, your attempts to introduce friends are met with baseless accusations of infidelity.

Never Hang Out With Your People

A partner invested in a future with you engages with your circle. On the other hand, narcissists only see you as a controlling toy and avoid interactions with your family and friends.

Dislike Anything You Like

You'll observe that the narcissist's initial resonance with your interests slowly turns into disdain. The narcissist tests control by disliking what you cherish, attempting to reshape your preferences. They once shared your enthusiasm for a show but now criticize it, insisting on aligning your tastes with theirs.

Monologues About Themselves

Narcissists navigate conversations with an inflated sense of self-importance. Every dialogue turns into a self-centered monologue, ignoring your feelings and requests. Discussions become one-sided, revolving solely around their achievements and desires.

Admits About Their Traits

Proud of their toxic traits, narcissists may openly acknowledge their manipulative, self-centered nature. They boast about being toxic or narcissistic, considering it a point of pride. You are mistaken if you assume that their acknowledgment implies a willingness to change.

Always Negative

A constant negative outlook, especially from covert narcissists, is a red flag. Insecure and seeking validation, they promote negativity to avoid loss or shame. They consistently express pessimism, fearing the repercussions of even minor events.

Always Try to Cross Your Boundaries

Testing your boundaries becomes a sinister game for narcissists. They push buttons to gauge your strength, starting with seemingly harmless actions. For instance, they intentionally violate a known boundary, dismissing your anger or distress as an over-reaction.

As we reflect on the complications of those ensnared in narcissistic relationships, we are now prepared to venture deeper into the labyrinth and explore the impact of narcissistic abuse on individuals.

CHAPTER 2
THE ANATOMY OF A TARGET

Living with a narcissist is like living in a constant self-doubt bubble; it's like you're never enough of anything and constantly questioning yourself.

ANONYMOUS

Nestled in the enchanting landscape of the Hollywood Hills, Ronia Fraser was living her California dream life as the finance head of a multinational corporation worth millions. With a thriving career, a beautiful home, and the allure of sunny California, Ronia had it all. It was a life that made her feel like she was on top of the world.

Ronia's life took an unexpected turn when she met a man who, at first, seemed too good to be true. Little did she know that a chance meeting at a party would set the stage for her descent into the abyss of narcissistic abuse. Her initial feelings of being cherished and understood were transformed into a nightmare as her partner's manipulative tactics took hold.

As the relationship evolved, Ronia was subjected to love bombing, emotional roller coasters, and gaslighting. She watched in despair as her sense of reality crumbled, replaced by the chaotic narrative spun by her abuser. She even began to question her worth.

Throughout her harrowing experience, Ronia grappled with her unwavering belief in the love she once knew. It's a journey that exposes the insidious nature of narcissistic abuse, where the abuser skillfully maintains a facade of charm in public while, behind closed doors, the victim's life is dismantled, block by block.

In the end, Ronia's resilience led her on a path of recovery, embracing various therapeutic techniques to heal the deep wounds of narcissistic abuse. Her transformation into a trauma recovery coach is a testament to the strength of survivors, and her dedication to helping others recover and rediscover themselves is a beacon of hope in the darkness.

EXPLORING THE VICTIM'S POINT OF VIEW: WHY ME?

In the shadowy world of narcissistic and sociopathic abuse, victims often find themselves grappling with a profound and perplexing question: Why me? Their suffering, meticulously concealed behind the mask of their abusers, is a complex tapestry of trauma and psychological manipulation. To delve into the mindset of these victims and understand the reasons they give themselves, let's explore their experiences through the lens of real-life examples (Arabi, 2017).

The Charismatic Mask of the Abuser

One compelling reason victims question their own judgment is the charismatic facade of their abusers. Narcissists and sociopaths are skilled at projecting a persona of charm, composure, and likability, fooling not only their victims but society at large. Victims often ask themselves, "Why did I keep suffering? Why couldn't I see through their facade?"

Traumatic Bond and Fear of Retaliation

The victims of covert psychological abuse often endure in silence due to the profound trauma bond they develop with their abusers. This bond, woven through intense emotional experiences, can feel impossible to break (Lancer, 2020). The fear of retaliation adds another layer to their suffering, leaving them questioning their choices: "Why can't I break free? Why do I protect my abuser?"

In a chilling narrative, a former United States Air Force veteran and his wife fell victim to relentless bullying and harassment by a narcissistic tormentor. This tormentor employed smear campaigns, job loss, financial account hacking, and cyberstalking to prey on the couple. The resultant trauma led to the creation of "Shane's Law," a petition aimed at legally protecting victims from these underhanded bullying methods. Despite their ordeal, the victims still struggled to sever ties with their abuser, their hesitance stemming from their profound bond and fear of repercussions.

The Myth of "Mutual Abuse" and Victim-Blaming

Society's misconceptions about abusive relationships deepen the suffering of victims. The misguided notion of "mutual abuse," where both parties are deemed responsible, can lead victims to blame themselves. They grapple with the question, "Did I contribute to the abuse? Was I partially to blame?"

Malignant narcissists excel at manipulation and gaslighting, leaving their victims in a constant state of self-doubt. The abusers skillfully engineer situations that provoke reactions from their victims, which they then exploit as proof of their victims' instability. This manipulation perpetuates a twisted narrative, causing victims to question their own role in the abuse.

THE EMPATH-NARCISSIST CONNECTION: AN INTRIGUING ATTRACTION

Why do narcissists and empaths, seemingly polar opposites, find themselves inexplicably drawn to each other? It's a perplexing question that defies easy explanation. The interplay between these two personality types is a complex dance, rooted in psychological factors that reveal an intricate tapestry of human behavior. Let's explore this fascinating connection between empaths and narcissists (Burgemeester, 2022).

The Narcissist's Thirst for Attention

One cornerstone of narcissism is an insatiable need for attention. Narcissists thrive on being the center of the universe, requiring constant admiration and praise. They bask in the spotlight, whether it's an audience of one or a crowd. They feed off the attention they receive, and their egos swell with each affirmation (Koprowski, 2023).

Reliance on External Validation

Beyond mere attention, narcissists rely heavily on external validation for their sense of self-worth. Their self-esteem is not derived from within but depends on the affirmation they receive from others. This twisted sense of reality demands constant validation to maintain their inflated self-image. This need dovetails perfectly with the empath's inclination to provide unwavering support and affirmation.

The Role of Empathy in Manipulation

Both empaths and narcissists share a common trait: empathy. However, their types of empathy differ significantly. Research reveals that narcissists score highly in cognitive empathy, allowing them to recognize and understand emotions in others. Empaths, conversely, excel in emotional empathy, which means they deeply feel the emotions of others.

Narcissists Target Vulnerability

Narcissists, with their high cognitive empathy, excel at identifying vulnerable individuals. They observe potential victims dispassionately, with the intent to target them. Empaths, characterized by their caring and attentive nature, become prime targets, offering the narcissists the devotion they crave.

The Initial Facade of Narcissistic Kindness

Narcissists strategically present an illusion of kindness, often during the initial stages of a relationship. They study their target, pinpointing vulnerabilities and utilizing manipulative tactics such as love bombing. The sudden display of affection and charm knocks victims off their feet. However, the abrupt shift from charm to manipulation occurs when the victim is already deeply emotionally invested.

Quick Descent Into Love

Empaths, driven by their emotional nature, swiftly fall in love when they sense attraction from others. Their heightened emotional sensitivity enables them to perceive subtle cues of affection. Narcissists exploit this tendency by presenting affection, faux love, and love bombing early in the relationship, prompting empaths to fall in love quickly.

Self-Blame in Relationships

Empaths tend to be hard on themselves and often shoulder the blame for relationship failures. They possess a deep understanding of human nature's frailties and are more forgiving. In times of strife, empaths are quicker to forgive their partners and find fault within themselves.

In essence, empaths embrace the role of the "fixer" in relationships, driven by their compassionate nature. This tendency to blame themselves and their desire to mend any relationship problems keep them trapped.

Fulfilling Mutual Needs

In their intricate connection, narcissists and empaths create a co-dependent relationship. Narcissists require love and attention, while empaths thrive on being needed. This illusion of being in a mutually beneficial relationship hurts the empaths in the long run.

CHILDHOOD TRAUMAS AND PREDISPOSITION TO NARCISSISTIC ALLURE

If you've ever questioned the connection between your painful childhood experiences and later enduring narcissistic abuse as an adult, you're not alone. Many individuals find themselves drawn into relationships with narcissists, often due to underlying psychological factors rooted in early trauma. Narcissists exploit these emotional wounds, using them as entry points for manipulation. Let's delve into the psychological reasons behind how childhood traumas can affect victims and explore the intricacies of this connection.

The Impact of Childhood Trauma: The Inability to Cope

Trauma stems from an inability to effectively deal with overwhelming and stressful situations. It occurs when we struggle to process difficult emotions and lack the means to find a resolution. This unprocessed trauma becomes ingrained within our emotional and nervous systems, influencing our emotions, thoughts, and, ultimately, every aspect of our lives.

The Role of Trauma in Shaping Beliefs

Trauma is the driving force behind many belief systems that form our inner identity. Traumatic beliefs become our reality and lead to self-fulfilling prophecies, causing us to repeat the same patterns and disappointments, even when we try to avoid them. This phenomenon is particularly evident in cases of narcissistic abuse, where victims find themselves ensnared in traumatic patterns that defy reason.

The Impact of Epigenetics: Ancestral Trauma

The ability of certain genes to switch on or off is inherited, according to the science of epigenetics. If our ancestors experienced trauma, these epigenetic factors could predispose us to issues with right-brain development and stress handling from birth. These factors may lead to an overactive amygdala, which prevents us from anchoring into our core identity to manage stress effectively.

The Chain Reaction: How Dissociation in Childhood Leads to Ongoing Trauma

When caregivers fail to provide the emotional support needed to integrate stressful experiences into calm and safety, children lack the inner resources to cope independently. This results in traumatic cycles of feeling overwhelmed by unprocessed emotions, accompanied by feelings of shame, guilt, and self-blame for having these emotions.

Complex Post-Traumatic Stress Disorder (CPTSD): A Vicious Cycle

Complex post-traumatic stress disorder (CPTSD) is a recurring, chronic sense of unsafety, primarily due to the inability to feel at home within oneself. The inability to find self-worth, self-love, self-value, and resilience in the face of difficulties is what characterizes CPTSD and causes a profound sense of powerlessness.

Narcissistic Allure and Childhood Traumas: The Connection

If you felt unloved during your childhood, it's essential to understand how these experiences can lead to attracting partners with narcissistic tendencies in adulthood. Unloved daughters, in particular, may find themselves drawn to partners with narcissistic traits. Several reasons underlie this phenomenon:

a. **Familiar Manipulation:** If you manipulation and control in your childhood, you may find abusive dynamics familiar and, unfortunately, be more likely to accept them in your adult relationships.

b. **Normalization of Verbal Abuse:** Childhood experiences can normalize verbal abuse, making it more acceptable in adult relationships. This can perpetuate patterns of low self-esteem and poor self-respect.

c. **Mistaking Game-Playing for Excitement:** You may mistake the emotional rollercoaster of game-playing and anxiety for passion, which often fuels narcissistic relationships.

d. **Gaslighting and Validation:** If you were invalidated or gaslighted as a child, you might tolerate similar experiences in your adult relationships.

PERSONALITY TRAITS THAT NARCISSISTS ARE DRAWN TO

If you've ever wondered why narcissists are drawn to certain people, it's not just about attention; it's a nuanced set of personality traits they seek. Understanding these traits sheds light on the dynamics of relationships with narcissists. Let's delve into some prominent traits that make a person attractive to a narcissist:

1. **Feeling Responsible for Others:** Narcissists crave partners who feel responsible for their emotional well-being. Despite the common belief that they have colossal egos, narcissists, at their core, are insecure. They rely on their partners to constantly reinforce their importance and value.

2. **Sacrificing Their Own Emotional Needs:** Partners who prioritize others' needs over their own are ideal for narcissists. In a relationship with a narcissist, there often isn't enough space for the partner's needs due to the narcissist's extensive emotional demands.

3. **Highly Empathetic:** Empathy is a potent lure for narcissists. Individuals with high empathy make perfect targets because they provide the acknowledgment and validation narcissists crave. Highly empathetic partners genuinely care for others' feelings, making narcissists feel valued and special.

4. **Complex Self-Esteem:** Narcissists are attracted to partners with a mix of high and low self-esteem. These partners appear confident but harbor pockets of self-doubt, often stemming from early experiences. This combination aligns with the narcissist's need for a dynamic and appealing image.

5. **Sacrificing Their Self-Image:** Narcissists meticulously craft their self-image. In choosing a partner, they seek someone who enhances and supports the image they wish to present to the world. It's a calculated and transactional selection process to fulfill their needs.

6. **Prone to Guilt:** Narcissists favor individuals prone to feeling guilty. Those who doubt themselves in emotionally complex situations become easier to manipulate and control. Narcissists believe that guilt-prone individuals are less likely to leave them, contributing to their need for control.

7. **Loyalty:** Narcissists crave unwavering loyalty. They want to believe you'll stand by them, no matter how they treat you. Unfortunately, this loyalty is often a one-way street, and once they've drained a relationship, they're ready to move on.

8. **Non-Questioning Nature:** The fragile ego of a narcissist can't withstand scrutiny. They prefer a partner who doesn't question their actions or feelings, allowing them the freedom to do as they wish without consequences.

9. **Forgiveness:** Easy forgiveness is a green light for abusers. Narcissists seldom change, relying on a forgiving partner who accepts apologies and gestures without demanding substantial behavioral shifts.

10. **Passivity:** Total control is a narcissist's preference. They seek a pliant partner, someone passive who goes along with their desires. Attention and praise for taking charge in the relationship are crucial for their satisfaction.

PSYCHOLOGICAL TOLL OF NARCISSISTIC ABUSE ON THE VICTIM

The psychological toll of narcissistic abuse on the victim is profound and multifaceted, impacting both mental and physical well-being. The effects of narcissistic abuse can be categorized into various dimensions, shedding light on the extensive reach of this form of emotional manipulation (Relojo-Howell, 2022).

Physical Manifestations of Trauma

Imagine your brain on high alert, with a constant rush of adrenaline and cortisol coursing through your veins. It's not a fleeting response to danger but a relentless state, triggered by the sustained stress of narcissistic abuse. Constant exposure to narcissistic abuse and stress results in cardiovascular diseases knocking on your door, the unwelcome companionship of obesity, arthritis, high blood pressure, type 2 diabetes, and the shackles of substance dependency and behavioral addictions.

Psychological Toll of Narcissistic Abuse

Exposure to extreme narcissism erases your identity, fostering psycho-emotional turmoil. Imagine a maze where your identity is the prize and narcissistic abuse is the architect. Manipulation, coercion, and the violation of your boundaries force you into a never-ending dance of fight, flight, freeze, or fawn responses (Cuncic, 2023). This array of emotions leads to a haunting symphony of mental health conditions—major depressive disorder, generalized anxiety disorder, and the lingering echoes of post-traumatic stress disorder (PTSD).

Impact on Self-Worth and Identity – Establishing the Need for Healing

Narcissistic abuse instills a sense of worthlessness and inferiority in victims. The erasure of identity and constant criticism lead to self-doubt, feelings of defectiveness, and an inability to assert oneself. You may struggle with decision-making, experience low self-esteem, and grapple with shame and embarrassment. The journey to rebuilding involves recognizing and accepting your feelings. It's about embracing self-care, connecting with the essence of who you truly are, and, most importantly, learning to trust yourself again (Dawson, 2023).

Financial Impact

Financial abuse, a prominent feature of narcissistic abuse, involves sabotaging your income through manipulation and control. The fallout extends beyond wallets, echoing in the corridors of physical and mental health—a phenomenon known as allostatic load.

Recovery and Self-Care

Envision a healing horizon where the focus shifts from the narcissistic storm to the calm within. It starts with activities that bring peace—realistic health goals, time management skills, nourishing your body, and embracing 30 minutes of movement every day. It's about restful sleep, moments with loved ones, mindfulness, and carving out time for hobbies. Recovery is not just possible; it's a journey of reclaiming your life—one step, one day at a time.

GROWING BEYOND THE PAIN OF NARCISSISTIC ABUSE

Embarking on a transformative journey beyond the pain of narcissistic abuse involves confronting various challenges. Picture a world where victimhood becomes an all-encompassing identity, driving an insatiable need for attention and approval. The lingering effects of numbed emotions post-abuse can dull empathy, leading to inadvertent abusive behaviors. Children, especially the vulnerable, absorb these influences profoundly.

Yet, amid these challenges, the positive note rings true: transformation is possible with therapy and time, offering hope for shedding undesirable traits and crafting a unique journey to healing and growth.

Unlocking Resilience After Narcissistic Abuse

After narcissistic abuse, rediscovering the full spectrum of your emotions is key. Suppressing difficult feelings hinders your ability to embrace the positive ones. Imagine resilience as a muscle, gaining strength through acknowledging and navigating through the entire range of emotions.

Remember, resilience isn't about sustained intensity but adapting to the unexpected. Accept change, acknowledge accomplishments, and rebuild your support network. Developing resilience is a journey of self-connection, providing the tools to face challenges and thrive after abuse.

The importance of building resilience can't be stressed enough because of the benefits it offers (Nichols, 2023):

1. **Breaking the Cycle of Adversity:** Resilience isn't about bouncing back effortlessly; it's about the tenacity to transcend trauma over time. Research on resilience amid narcissistic abuse reveals that individuals can break the cycle of adversity by refusing to let a difficult past dictate their future.

2. **Transforming Pain Into Power:** Resilience provides a silver lining to the aftermath of narcissistic abuse. Those who have overcome such trauma often report a profound sense of self-improvement and personal growth. By harnessing their resilience, survivors not only heal but also emerge as stronger, kinder individuals, driven to make a positive impact on themselves and the world around them.

3. **Mental Health Sanctuary:** Resilience and mental well-being intertwine; it's crucial for lowering stress, anxiety, and depression. Developing resilience enables you to navigate challenges constructively, fostering a positive outlook and emotional balance.

4. **Empowerment Through Resilience:** Cultivating resilience is not just a skill but an empowerment after

narcissistic abuse. It strengthens problem-solving, enhances relationships, and serves as a shield against mental health disorders.

Sharing Stories of Individuals Moving Beyond Their Traumas

Story 1: Clara's Liberation

For three grueling years, Clara found herself ensnared in the web of a charming but sinister figure named Ethan. He wasn't just a narcissist; his whispers hinted at sociopathy and psychopathy, leaving Clara's self-worth in tatters. Friends and family begged her to escape this toxic entanglement, but love, or what she believed to be love, shackled her.

Ethan played a twisted game, alternating between lifting Clara to euphoric heights and ruthlessly stomping her down. The cycle left her questioning her sanity and value. She believed in the good, even as the bad piled up like a tower of cards. The darkest revelation came when she realized that Ethan's happiness peaked when he held her beneath his controlling thumb.

Summoning the strength to stand up for herself became the tipping point. However, liberation came at a cost—Ethan's wrath erupted into physical violence. He reveled in painting Clara as the "crazy" one online, his friends echoing the mockery. The toll was severe; Clara's heart, both figuratively and literally, bore the scars of her torment.

Yet Clara's story didn't end in the depths of despair. It rose from the ashes of pain. Her resilience became the beacon guiding her through the labyrinth of healing. The turning point arrived through an online test that unveiled the insidious truth about her tormentor. Clara emerged not just as a survivor but as a warrior, fighting not only to break free but also to reclaim her shattered self. The path to forgiveness, especially for herself, was an ongoing struggle, a testament to the enduring strength it takes to rebuild after narcissistic captivity.

Story 2: Olivia's Phoenix Rise

Love, for Olivia, wore the deceptive cloak of conditional affection. Her husband, a master of control and manipulation, spun tales designed to make her doubt herself. The journey to self-discovery was a painful unraveling of gaslighting and deceit that kept her ensnared.

It took relentless inner work for Olivia to free herself from the suffocating narratives. Three years after the tumultuous exit, she looked back with gratitude for those agonizing first steps. Co-parenting presented a perennial challenge, but Olivia's resilience grew with each trial, a testament to the strength she discovered within.

The realization struck her belatedly—her ex-husband's need for control transcended his own desires. It was about keeping her engaged and ensuring he held the strings to influence her life. The goalposts moved incessantly, and Olivia understood that as long as she played the game, resolution would remain elusive. The final act involved cutting him out, a drastic yet necessary measure to salvage her own peace.

Olivia's tale echoed the sentiments of many survivors who, in hindsight, discovered the insidious nature of narcissistic manipulation. The journey from victim to survivor was a metamorphosis, marked by the strength to redefine love and rebuild a life free from the shackles of a narcissist's influence. Olivia's resilience became the driving force, turning her story into a testament of triumph over adversity.

QUIZ: AM I SUFFERING FROM TRAUMA?

Please answer the following questions honestly by choosing the response that best reflects your experiences:

1. How do you typically react to stress or unexpected challenges?

A) I manage stress well and can adapt easily.
B) I sometimes struggle but generally cope with stress.
C) I often feel overwhelmed, and stress affects me deeply.

2. How would you describe your sleep patterns?

A) I consistently get restful and uninterrupted sleep.
B) My sleep is occasionally disrupted, but I generally get enough rest.
C) I frequently experience nightmares, insomnia, or restless sleep

3. In your relationships, do you find it challenging to trust others?

A) I generally trust people and believe in the goodness of others.

B) I am cautious about trust but can open up over time.

C) I struggle to trust and often fear betrayal in relationships.

4. How do you perceive your emotional responses to past traumatic events?

A) I have processed and come to terms with past traumas.

B) I still grapple with some emotions related to past events.

C) Past traumas significantly impact my daily emotions and functioning.

5. Reflecting on your self-worth, how would you describe your feelings about yourself?

A) I generally have a positive and stable sense of self-worth.

B) I sometimes doubt myself, but I can build confidence.

C) I often struggle with feelings of worthlessness and inadequacy.

As we delve deeper into the process of recovery, we now turn our focus to the intricate interplay between the mind and the heart, exploring the neurological impacts of abuse.

CHAPTER 3
THE SCIENCE BEHIND RECOVERY

In the intricate dance of our minds, trauma can be an uninvited choreographer, reshaping the very stage on which our thoughts and emotions perform. Imagine your brain as a complex orchestra, with each neuron playing a crucial note in the symphony of your daily life. Trauma, on the other hand, is like a jarring melody that disrupts the harmony and causes emotional damage.

Trauma can change your brain on many levels, from the way you make decisions to your immediate, subconscious responses to the world around you. Part of the reason it can be so hard to overcome the effects of trauma is that it goes after several areas of your brain at once. Ongoing stress and fear shrink and impact brain functions and require a long period of neurogenesis and brain healing via therapy, a changed environment, and a brain-healthy approach to counteract.

To heal from emotional abuse, it's essential to learn the nuances of the mental and physical effects of trauma. This chapter is your guide to exploring the science that underpins the journey of recovery from narcissistic abuse.

TRAUMA VS. POST TRAUMATIC STRESS DISORDER

Trauma and post-traumatic stress disorder (PTSD) are like inter-connected puzzle pieces, reshaping our brain chemistry in response to life's upheavals. PTSD changes the structures and functioning of your brain, affecting the delicate balance of neuro-transmitters and hormones. While many associate PTSD with military combat, it can emerge from various traumas, including sexual abuse.

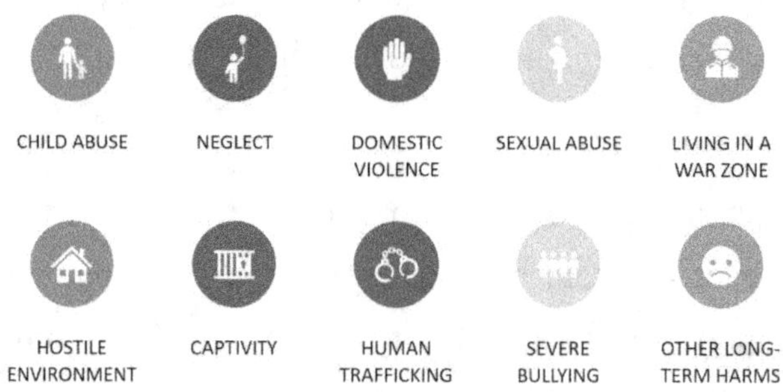

Figure 3. Potential causes of PSTD (Source: Wikimedia, Creative Commons)

Consider this snapshot of life's impact: 49% of rape victims, almost a third of severe assault survivors, and 16.8% of those in serious accidents develop PTSD. The echoes continue—15.4% of shooting or stabbing victims, 14.3% facing sudden loss, and 10.4% of parents with seriously ill children find themselves grappling with PTSD. Even witnessing severe harm to another person affects 7.3% of individuals, while 3.8% of those who endure natural disasters bear the weight of PTSD. These stats reveal a diverse array of triggers, each potentially leading to a unique journey through trauma's intricate dance (Melissa, 2023).

The impact of PSTD extends beyond the brain, showing up in physical changes. The immune system transforms, inflammation becomes widespread, and physical echoes of trauma—muscle aches, sleep issues, gastrointestinal problems, and high blood pressure—emerge. Understanding PTSD leads to intervention. Therapies like cognitive behavioral therapy and medications, coupled with coping strategies like active coping, nervous system checkups, and mindfulness practices, become sentinels against the onslaught of PTSD.

NEUROLOGICAL IMPACTS OF ABUSE

Navigating the labyrinth of emotional abuse isn't just about recognizing visible scars; it's about understanding the intricate impacts on your mind, relationships, self-image, and well-being. Emotional abuse, often camouflaged by subtle tactics like gaslighting and shaming, aims to render you powerless and hopeless. Whether encountered in fleeting interactions or endured across years, the effects are real, leaving imprints on your emotional, physical, and mental health.

How the Brain Responds to Emotional Trauma?

According to a 2006 study by the National Institutes of Health (NIH), our brain is like a trio—the emotional center (amygdala), memory maestro (hippocampus), and regulator of emotions (prefrontal cortex)—working together to manage stress (Smith, 2021). When reminded of a traumatic experience, our brain's trio orchestrates stress management, often intensifying reactions to reminders of the trauma. This heightened emotional response stems from the amygdala's hyperactivity, the hippocampus's struggle to distinguish between actual events and memories, and the prefrontal cortex's difficulty regulating emotions. Despite these challenges, the brain possesses remarkable adaptability. Neuroplasticity, the ability to form new connections, becomes a beacon of hope for recovery.

Trauma Bonding Explained

Trauma bonding, as coined by Patrick Carnes, reveals the complex attachment an abused person forms with their abuser, especially in cyclical abuse patterns. This bond arises from a mix of abuse and positive reinforcement, with the abuser professing love and remorse after each incident. The victim, experiencing feelings of love and dependence, struggles to leave the abusive situation, facing confusion and dependency. The seven stages of trauma bonding include love bombing, gaining trust, criticism, manipulation, resignation, distress, and repetition (Zoppi, 2023).

Signs of trauma bonding encompass covering up abuse, blaming oneself, and cycles of promises to change. Common in various abusive situations, trauma bonding is not irreversible, and remedies like desensitization therapy and trauma-focused cognitive behavioral therapy offer hope for breaking the bond.

Changes in Neural Pathways Post-Abuse

When children face early childhood neglect or abuse, their developing brains undergo significant changes in neural connections as adaptations to adverse experiences (Bremner, 2006). Our brain's plasticity allows for recovery through sensitive, nurturing care and positive influences. A baby's brain, initially comprising millions of neurons connected by synapses, builds billions of new synaptic connections through experiences. The brain's pruning process strengthens used synapses while discarding unused ones, enhancing efficiency. Sensitive and critical periods in brain development underscore the impact of experiences on neural pathways.

A child's response to neglect or abuse involves adaptations rather than irreparable damage, leading to hyper-vigilance and maladaptive responses. Chronic stress triggers physiological responses, impacting the amygdala, hippocampus, and prefrontal cortex, which are crucial for emotional regulation, higher cognitive functions, and self-regulation. High-quality nurturing care and positive experiences can repair earlier damage. The concept of differential susceptibility acknowledges genetic variations in children's responses to caregiving environments, influencing the success of interventions. Individualized parenting and support, along with everyday tasks reinforcing positive pathways, play pivotal roles in helping your child overcome adversities and rebuild neural connections after abuse.

PSYCHOLOGICAL HEALING MECHANISMS

Our brain, a versatile superhero, employs neuroplasticity—a power enabling it to rewire and adapt. Think of it as a mental renovation, rebuilding pathways damaged by adversity. Psychological healing mechanisms are the superheroes of our mental well-being, working behind the scenes to mend the wounds in our minds. Imagine them as the quiet architects of resilience and growth. Let's dive into the most effective healing mechanisms!

The Role of Therapy

In the labyrinth of life, when faced with the monsters of crisis, anxiety, or depression, therapy emerges as a guiding light—a beacon of hope. Wondering if therapy is your superhero along this journey? You're not alone. Many find solace in therapy, especially when navigating significant crises or prolonged periods of emotional turbulence. Your mental health journey is unique, and the therapy that fits is the one that resonates with you. Seek support that feels like the right fit for your needs (Lindberg, 2020).

Talk Therapy: Your Dialogue With Healing

Talk therapy is a dynamic tool wielded by mental health experts such as psychiatrists, psychologists, and therapists. It's not a one-size-fits-all solution but a versatile approach that encourages open and honest conversations. According to the American Psychological Association, about 75 percent of those who embark on this therapeutic journey witness its transformative benefits.

Talk therapy's magic lies in its ability to address a spectrum of concerns—from stress management and relationship problems to the realms of depression and anxiety disorders. It opens the door for communication, a powerful force that shapes our mental landscapes.

Individual Therapy: Your Personal Exploration Space

In the realm of therapy, individual sessions create a haven for self-exploration. It's not couples, families, or groups—it's just you. Imagine a safe space where you delve into your thoughts, feelings, and concerns, like a tailor stitching a bespoke suit for your mental well-being.

The goal of individual therapy is clear: inspire change and enhance the quality of life through self-awareness. It's a journey tailored solely for you, fostering not just change but also empowerment. Here, you develop improved communication skills, gain insights into your life, and craft coping strategies to navigate life's twists and turns.

Family Therapy: Untangling Knots Together

When family hurdles seem insurmountable, family therapy steps in. It's not about fixing one person; it's about healing the family unit. With a focus on relationships, family therapy dives into the intricate dynamics that weave the familial fabric.

Picture a therapist addressing mental and emotional disorders, behavioral problems, and relationship issues within the family system. It's about improving communication, treating mental health concerns, fostering collaboration, and equipping individuals with coping strategies. It's the art of healing collectively.

Cognitive-Behavioral Therapy (CBT): Rewiring Thought Patterns

Cognitive-behavioral therapy (CBT), a fusion of behavioral and cognitive therapies, is a targeted approach used to tackle conditions like anxiety disorders, depression, and more. Think of it as a mental renovation—rewiring thought patterns for a healthier mindset.

Research attests to CBT's success in reducing depression levels, managing bipolar disorder, and consistently supporting those grappling with anxiety disorders. It's a strategic ally against the battles within the mind.

Physical Brain Neurogenesis

Imagine your brain as a dynamic city constantly under construction, where new neurons are the architects of recovery. Engaging in activities like exercise, mindfulness, and learning becomes your toolkit for scaffolding this reconstruction process. These activities aren't just pastimes; they are the builders mending the neural pathways, allowing your brain to forge new connections and rise, phoenix-like, from the ashes of adversity. Your brain, the ultimate architect, crafts its renewal, proving that healing is not just a concept but a tangible, intricate dance of neurogenesis (Schoenfeld & Cameron, 2014).

SSRIs and Other Medications in Brain Healing

Traditional views often paint depression as a chemical puzzle, with medications like SSRIs aiming to boost those neurotransmitter levels. But there's more to the story! Recent research dives deep into the brain's inner workings during stress, depression, and antidepressant treatment. Stress shakes up your brain, causing changes like losing dendritic spines. Antidepressants, especially SSRIs, act like brain guardians, shielding against and even undoing some of these changes. It's like they're flipping a switch back to a healthier brain setting, helping you adapt and learn.

Diet for Neurogenesis – The MIND Diet

Ever heard of the MIND diet? It's not just about what you eat; it's about feeding your brain with the right information. Researchers are buzzing about its potential to trim waistlines and boost your brainpower. This diet seems to have a sweet spot—it works its magic when the numbers on the scale start shifting. In a world grappling with obesity and its effects on our brains, the MIND diet steps in as a hero, focusing on reducing stress and tweaking structural functions. It's like a brain-friendly superhero diet, and we're just beginning to uncover its cognitive superpowers.

Exercise, Sleep, and Other Strategies for Neurogenesis

Guess what's as good for your brain as it is for your body? Exercise! It's not just about the muscles; it's about growing new neurons, too. Picture this: your brain cells doing jumping jacks in excitement. And mental workouts are the anti-aging elixir when it comes to aging brains. Keep that brain flexing by learning new, challenging skills. Oh, and don't underestimate the power of a good night's sleep—it's like a superhero swooping in to regulate stress hormones and keep your neurogenesis in check. Meditation, a bit of romance, and a diet rich in brain-boosting goodies like flavonoids and omega-3s? It's like a party for your neurons! Just remember, these are more like brain boosters, not FDA-approved brain builders. We're still decoding the brain's secret language.

Recommended Therapy Techniques

Let's uncover the magic of different therapy techniques to take control of our lives.

Cognitive Behavioral Therapy (CBT)

CBT is your personalized toolkit for rewiring the way you think and feel. It's like having a mental renovation crew that identifies and swaps out those old, faulty thought patterns for shiny, new ones (Cherry, 2023). Picture it as a journey into your mind, where you learn to challenge negativity, set goals, and solve problems like a pro. But where's the CBT magic? It's in the techniques—from goal-setting gymnastics to the art of self-monitoring, you're not just talking about feelings; you're also actively reshaping them. So, if you're ready to transform your thought patterns and tackle everything from addiction to relationship problems, CBT is your brain's workout routine for a healthier mindset.

Dialectical Behavior Therapy (DBT)

DBT is your emotional ninja training ground. Have you ever felt like your feelings are on a rollercoaster without seatbelts? DBT gives you the tools to navigate that wild ride. It's not just therapy; it's a crash course in emotion management. Imagine your mind as a dojo and DBT as the sensei teaching you mindfulness, distress tolerance, and emotion regulation. This isn't about just talking; it's about practical skills like setting boundaries, handling intense emotions, and mastering the art of interpersonal effectiveness. Suppose you're dealing with tough stuff like borderline personality disorder, self-harm, or anxiety. In that case, DBT is your emotional martial arts class, empowering you to face life's challenges with resilience and strength (Taylor, 2011).

Multimodal Therapy (MMT): A Symphony of Healing

In the world of psychotherapy, multimodal therapy (MMT) stands out as a symphony of approaches, captivating the complexities of the human mind (Lazarus, 2018). Imagine therapy not as a one-size-fits-all solution but as a tailored ensemble, where various therapeutic techniques harmonize to treat the whole person, not just the symptoms. Crafted by psychologist

Arnold Lazarus in the 1960s, MMT, also known as eclectic or integrative psychotherapy, recognizes that one modality may not suffice. The term "modality" refers to different treatment methods, such as cognitive therapy, behavior therapy, and psychoanalysis—each unraveling a unique facet of a person's psychological tapestry. However, like any symphony, MMT requires a skilled conductor—therapists with a broad repertoire of psychological approaches, ensuring no note is missed.

Rational Emotive Behavior Therapy (REBT)

Conceived by Dr. Albert Ellis in the 1950s, REBT is a beacon for those navigating the turbulent seas of depression, anxiety, and various emotional storms (Raypole, 2018). At its core, REBT revolves around the ABCs: activating events, beliefs, and consequences. Picture a scenario where a text goes unanswered. The activating event (A) triggers irrational beliefs (B), leading to distressing consequences (C). REBT's problem-solving strategies address activating events, cognitive restructuring transforms irrational beliefs, and coping techniques soothe the emotional aftermath. REBT doesn't just treat the symptoms; it dissects the layers, addressing secondary symptoms like anxiety about anxiety or depression about depression.

Mindfulness: A Sanctuary for Healing

Mindfulness is not just a practice; it's a sanctuary. For abuse victims, it becomes a haven where the tumultuous waters of the past find stillness. Through mindfulness, we learn to anchor ourselves in the present moment, away from the haunting specters of what was.

The healing potential of mindfulness lies in its ability to foster self-compassion. Picture a survivor acknowledging their emotions without judgment and embracing the wounded parts of themselves with kindness. It's a transformative journey from victimhood to empowerment.

As we delve deeper into the next chapter, "Charting the Road to Recovery," the role of mindfulness will unfurl with intricate details. It becomes a compass, guiding abuse victims through the labyrinth of healing, where each mindful step becomes a declaration: "I am reclaiming my narrative, one breath at a time."

Emily's Journey: Triumph Through Mindfulness

In the heartland of Illinois, Emily's story stands as a testament to the transformative power of mindfulness for narcissism victims. Battling the aftermath of a toxic relationship, Emily found herself ensnared in the tendrils of self-doubt and emotional wreckage. Mindfulness, however, emerged as her lifeline.

Haunted by persistent self-blame, Emily struggled to break free from the echoes of gaslighting. Mindfulness became her refuge, a space where she learned to observe her thoughts without succumbing to their destructive narratives. Through guided meditation, Emily confronted the shadows of manipulation, gradually unraveling the web that narcissistic abuse had woven around her.

In the crucible of mindfulness, Emily faced the daunting task of rebuilding her self-esteem. With each mindful breath, she shed the layers of doubt and reclaimed her autonomy. The practice became a daily ritual, a source of empowerment that allowed her to navigate the intricate path from victimhood to survivorship. Emily's story is a beacon for others, illustrating how mindfulness can be a powerful catalyst for healing in the aftermath of narcissistic trauma.

EMBRACING GROWTH

Reclaiming one's life after narcissistic abuse is similar to nurturing a garden after a storm. The soil, enriched by self-compassion, becomes the foundation for growth. Understanding post-traumatic growth becomes pivotal when we recognize and embrace new opportunities that arise from adversity. Psychologists Richard Tedeschi and Lawrence Calhoun identified five categories of growth, including forging stronger relationships, cultivating inner strength, gaining a deeper appreciation for life, and evolving spiritually. Post-traumatic growth doesn't negate the distress but asserts that it can coexist with post-traumatic stress disorder.

The Science Behind Resilience

Cultivating resilience involves recognizing the power of support systems—friends, therapists, or support groups—acting as pillars that weather the emotional storm. The consistent "serve and return" interactions between a child and a caregiver build the scaffolding for key capacities that enable children to respond to adversity and thrive. Resilience is born from a combination of internal disposition, external experiences, and positive relationships, contributing to healthy responses to stress (Walker & Salt, 2023). The science of resilience emphasizes the importance of coping with manageable threats and the malleability of resilience, dispelling the notion that it is an innate trait or a finite resource.

The Role of Support Systems and Social Networks

Social support systems and networks play a crucial role in brain neurogenesis, especially for survivors of narcissistic abuse. Beyond digital support, survivors benefit immensely from spaces like narcissistic abuse support groups, where they find validation, understanding, and a sense of community. These groups provide a safe haven for survivors to share their experiences, reinforcing the understanding that they are not alone. The journey to recovery involves embracing growth through understanding, resilience, and a robust support system, turning the tide from victimhood to survivorship.

A BRAIN-BOOSTING CHECKLIST FOR ABUSE SURVIVORS

Navigating the path to recovery from abuse involves not only emotional healing but also caring for your mental well-being. Consider a brain-boosting checklist designed to empower survivors to rebuild their lives (Kidd, 2022):

1. **Exercise Regularly:** Physical activity isn't just for your body; it's a powerful ally for your brain. Studies show that regular exercise enhances mental function and reduces the risk of Alzheimer's disease. Engage in activities like walking, swimming, or playing sports, aiming for 30 to 60 minutes several times a week.

2. **Prioritize Quality Sleep:** Sleep is a vital player in brain health. Aim for seven to eight consecutive hours of sleep per night to allow your brain to consolidate memories effectively. Quality sleep contributes to overall cognitive function and helps clear abnormal proteins in the brain.

3. **Adopt a Mediterranean Diet:** Your diet significantly impacts brain health. Embrace a Mediterranean diet rich in plant-based foods, whole grains, fish, and healthy fats like olive oil. This diet has been associated with a lower risk of Alzheimer's disease, emphasizing the importance of omega fatty acids for cognitive well-being.

4. **Stay Mentally Active:** Treat your brain like a muscle; use it regularly to keep it in shape. Engage in activities like crossword puzzles, reading, playing cards, or solving puzzles. Cross-training your brain with various activities enhances its effectiveness and resilience.

5. **Remain Socially Involved:** Combat isolation by fostering social connections. Social interaction helps ward off depression and stress, contributing to memory preservation. Actively seek opportunities to connect with loved ones, friends, and communities to strengthen your brain's health.

MINDFULNESS TECHNIQUES

Experiment with the following mindfulness techniques and find what resonates best with you (Ackerman, 2023). Remember, consistency is vital in mindfulness practice:

Technique	How-to Description
Mindful Breathing	Find a quiet space. Inhale slowly, counting to four. Hold briefly, then exhale for four counts. Focus on the breath, bringing your mind back when it wanders.
Body Scan Meditation	Lie down or sit comfortably. Mentally scan your body from head to toe, noticing sensations without judgment. Release tension as you exhale.
Guided Imagery	Close your eyes. Imagine a peaceful place. Engage all senses, noticing details. Breathe deeply, absorbing the calmness of your mental sanctuary.
Mindful Walking	Walk slowly, paying attention to each step. Feel the ground beneath your feet, notice your surroundings, and synchronize your breath with your steps.
Loving-Kindness Meditation	Focus on sending love and compassion. Begin with yourself, then extend it to others. Repeat phrases like "May you/I be happy, may you/I be healthy."
Mindful Eating	Eat slowly and deliberately. Pay attention to textures, flavors, and smells. Chew each bite thoroughly, savoring the experience without distractions.
Body Movement Mindfulness	Engage in mindful movements like yoga or tai chi. Focus on the sensations, breath, and the connection between your body and the movement.
5−4−3−2−1 Grounding Technique	Name five things you can see, four things you can touch, three things you can hear, two things you can smell, and one thing you can taste.
Breath Counting	Sit comfortably. Inhale naturally, exhale fully. Count each breath cycle up to ten, then start over. If your mind wanders, gently return to counting.
Gratitude Journaling	Write down things you're grateful for each day. Reflect on the positive aspects of your life, fostering a mindset of gratitude and appreciation.

As we conclude our exploration of the science behind recovery, it becomes evident that the amalgamation of mindfulness, psychological insights, and neurological understandings paves the way for a holistic approach to healing. Now, let's delve into Chapter 4: "Charting the Road to Recovery," where we'll navigate practical strategies and personalized pathways to empower survivors on their journey toward resilience and well-being.

CHAPTER 4
CHARTING THE ROAD TO RECOVERY

What man actually needs is not a tensionless state but rather the striving and struggling for some goal worthy of him. What he needs is not the discharge of tension at any cost, but the call of a potential meaning waiting to be fulfilled by him.

VIKTOR E. FRANKL

Today feels like a hesitant sunrise after a long, stormy night. For years, I've been lost in the labyrinth of someone else's desires, suffocated by the ever-tightening grip of a narcissistic relationship. But as the dawn breaks, I find myself standing on the threshold of something new—a chance at reclaiming the shattered pieces of myself.

My intuition whispered quietly for years that something was amiss. I silenced it, drowning its wisdom in the deafening applause of someone else's validation. But the whispers grew louder today, echoing the truth I'd been too scared to acknowledge. It was time to listen.

I sat with my feelings, acknowledging the knots in my stomach and the unease in my heart. The path to recovery demanded distance—physical and emotional. I learned the art of setting firm boundaries and creating a protective shield against manipulation. Reclaiming my personal space became a manifesto of self-liberation. I delved into the Grey Rock method, becoming as uninteresting to my abuser as an ordinary stone. The checklist on how to get away from a narcissist became my escape plan—a roadmap to freedom.

Grieving after the end of an abusive relationship became an emotional hangover, but I learned it was okay to feel conflicted. In the embrace of mindfulness, I found solace. Techniques, daily practices, and the wisdom of Eckhart Tolle became my companions on this healing journey.

As I document these initial steps in my diary, I feel a spark within myself. Today, I don't just survive; I strive for a life worthy of the warrior staring back at me in the mirror.

With hope,
Anna
Dated: November 24, 2019

Anna's diary entry unveils the raw emotions of a survivor stepping into the light after enduring the shadows of narcissistic abuse. The metaphorical storm has left its mark, but we witness a resilient spirit awakening through Anna's words.

As we delve into the next section, we will explore the intricacies of recognizing the need for change.

RECOGNIZING THE NEED FOR CHANGE

Emotional trauma, the silent intruder that leaves an indelible mark on our psyche, often lingers unnoticed until its symptoms emerge, affecting our daily lives. The journey toward recognizing the need for change begins with understanding the subtle signs echoing the aftermath of emotional trauma (Mason, 2023).

Navigating the Depths: The Interplay of Intuition and Trauma

In the realm of creation, artists describe their process as tapping into a source beyond conscious understanding—a sentiment mirrored in the intuitive whispers of our subconscious (Blackstock, 2023). Joseph Campbell's analogy of artists swimming in the ocean that psychotics drown in encapsulates the delicate dance between intuition and trauma, both originating in the subcortical brain. Trauma, etching imprints in the amygdala, disrupts intuition by amplifying hyperarousal and hypervigilance, drowning the subtler intuitive cues. Healing trauma becomes the key to unveiling intuition, a journey that restores trust, dismantles distorted beliefs, and fosters a genuine connection with the authentic self.

Embracing the Storm Within: The Power of Acknowledging Your Emotions

Imagine a symphony of emotions—some harmonious, others dissonant. When faced with the discordant notes of sadness, fear, or shame, the instinct is often to silence or drown them out. Yet, denying these emotions can lead to a turbulent sea within. The journey to emotional acceptance, akin to embracing the ebb and flow of a storm, holds the key to emotional regulation, fewer mood swings, and a restored equilibrium. Emotional acceptance is not surrendering to perpetual agony; it's like a soldier laying down arms after a long battle. While challenging, this acceptance becomes a beacon of self-compassion, steering you away from emotional turmoil.

Surviving the Abyss: Tales of Narcissistic Abuse Survivors

In the haunting aftermath of narcissistic abuse, the journey to survival often feels like navigating uncharted waters. Yet, there's a lighthouse in the distance, a glimmer of hope shared by those who've weathered the storm.

Melanie's Story

In the aftermath of surviving a harrowing experience of narcissistic abuse, Melanie's story unfolded against a backdrop of challenges that initially appeared insurmountable. The journey commenced with the subtle erosion of her self-esteem, orchestrated by the narcissist's meticulous crafting of a manipulative web. Gaslighting, emotional manipulation, and isolation became the daily battlegrounds where Melanie found herself entangled in a toxic cycle that seemed impervious to change.

However, within this darkness, pivotal turning points materialized. Melanie experienced a moment of clarity, a profound realization that the love she believed she was receiving was a distorted illusion. Empowered by this insight, she resolved to reclaim her narrative. Seeking support from friends, family, and professional therapists, she embarked on the courageous journey of unraveling the threads of manipulation that bound her.

The turning points in Melanie's narrative extended beyond escaping a toxic relationship; they were pivotal moments of change and self-discovery. She learned to set boundaries, prioritize self-care, and skillfully distinguish between genuine connections and manipulative tactics. The scars of her past transformed into symbols of strength, serving as a poignant reminder that she had not merely survived; she had embraced change and thrived.

Melaine's story transcended personal triumph; it became a guiding light for others grappling with similar challenges, a beacon of hope attesting that the imperative for change can lead to liberation from the shackles of narcissistic abuse.

Jo's Story

Jo faced a challenging upbringing marked by unrealistic expectations and constant criticism by her parents, which intricately wove a web of doubt around her self-worth. However, armed with resilience and an indomitable spirit, Jo navigated her way through the intricate challenges. Her techniques for overcoming the toxicity involved a profound journey of self-discovery and boundary-setting. Jo sought solace in therapy, where she learned to untangle the manipulative threads woven into the fabric of her identity. Establishing firm boundaries became a transformative act, allowing her to shield herself from the emotional onslaught and regain a sense of autonomy.

Jo's inspiration to break free emanated from within—a fierce desire to redefine her narrative and reclaim her intrinsic value. The process was arduous, manifested by self-doubt and the persistent echoes of past criticisms. However, each step forward was fueled by an inner flame of resilience—a refusal to be defined by the limitations imposed by a narcissistic relationship.

Triumph for Jo manifested itself in the gradual reconstruction of her self-esteem and the establishment of healthier relationships. The scars of the past became badges of honor, signifying not just survival but a triumphant ascent from the depths of emotional turmoil. Jo's story inspires others facing similar battles, illustrating that even in the aftermath of narcissistic relationships, the human spirit can emerge victorious, resilient, and capable of rewriting its own narrative.

STRATEGIES FOR DISTANCE

In the tumultuous odyssey of breaking free from the clutches of a narcissistic influence, picture emotional distancing as your personalized sanctuary—a potent act of self-preservation, not evasion. Think of it as your armor against the relentless emotional tempest conjured by narcissists. A seasoned psychotherapist, Jay Reid, likens navigating these relationships to a trail encounter with a rattlesnake (Reid, 2023). It's not avoidance; it's strategic sidestepping to ensure your survival.

Emotional and Physical Distancing

Emotional distance is your liberation ticket from the manipulative shackles of narcissists. You're not entangled in the emotional whirlwind they orchestrate when you're emotionally detached. With emotional distancing, you develop a resistance to manipulation and the strength to remain unaffected amid the storm. Recognize the red flags in your relationship. If you feel like you're walking on eggshells, if every conversation turns into a battleground, if guilt and exhaustion are your constant companions—it's your compass telling you it's time for emotional distance.

The labyrinth of narcissistic relationships demands not just emotional but physical distancing. It's time to take command. Picture the following strategies as your toolkit, empowering you to reclaim control over your life:

Limiting Contact: Your Shield Against Narcissistic Influence

To get out of a grinding cycle, aim to reduce the time you spend around narcissists and avoid situations fostering proximity—prioritize self-care. Even if you're still in a relationship with a narcissist, remember that you need to take care of yourself.

Identifying the Struggle

It's okay to acknowledge the difficulty of achieving physical distance. Narcissists are masters at manipulation. Background knowledge about the struggles of physical distancing empowers you to resist falling prey to emotional games. Acknowledging the guilt associated with distancing and remembering that it's about self-preservation is essential.

Refusing to Play the Games

Be prepared to refuse to play the games of narcissists. By not reacting emotionally, you're essentially taking away their power. Envision yourself reclaiming control by denying them the satisfaction of manipulating your emotions.

Maintaining Independence

Independence is your beacon of hope. Stand up for yourself, maintain your autonomy, and refuse to be controlled. It's your fortress against the narcissist's attempts to overpower and control. Picture yourself standing solid and unwavering in your commitment to self-preservation.

Acceptance: The Crucial Step in the Journey to Physical Distance

Acceptance is your crucial step. It is essential to confront the challenging reality—narcissists are incapable of change. See yourself redirecting your focus and liberating yourself from futile attempts to fix or alter the narcissist.

Setting Boundaries

Boundaries are your fortifications. Set firm limits and be unwavering in your commitment to self-preservation. Enforce these boundaries consistently to resist manipulation and keep the narcissist at arm's length.

Cultivate Honesty

Wield honesty as your weapon. Be honest about the narcissist's behavior and refuse to make excuses. It's time to recognize the manipulative patterns and stop explaining away their actions.

Awareness

Be vigilant about conversations and activities that trigger harm. Imagine yourself steering clear of situations designed by the narcissist to induce emotional turmoil. It's your navigation tool in the narcissistic minefield.

Setting Firm Boundaries: A Strategic Choice for Your Liberation

Imagine boundaries as the unyielding walls that safeguard your well-being amid the chaos of narcissistic relationships (Grande, 2023). These aren't mere lines drawn in the sand; they are your definitive stance against manipulation and deceit. Consider the intricate dance of asserting boundaries a strategic choice, a decisive move in reclaiming control over your life.

Anticipate resistance when setting boundaries with a narcissist. Be prepared for anger, manipulation, or complete disregard for your boundaries. While narcissists may not react well to being labeled, their awareness of how they're perceived doesn't necessarily alter their response to boundaries. Stand firm in asserting boundaries to reclaim control over your narrative in the narcissistic saga.

Rediscovering Personal Space and Autonomy

Imagine a sanctuary where your thoughts are sovereign and untouched by the manipulative echoes of narcissistic abuse. Reclaiming personal space and autonomy after enduring the relentless storm of narcissism is not just a journey; it's a courageous act of self-liberation. This quest involves drawing boundaries as bold as fortress walls. For instance, if the narcissist once dictated your every move, now is the time to decide when, where, and with whom you engage.

Let's delve into some of the powerful strategies for your liberation:

1. **Cultivate Personal Hobbies:** Dive into activities that define you outside the shadow of the narcissist. Whether painting, hiking, or playing an instrument, your hobbies are your exclusive retreat for fostering individuality.
2. **Forge Supportive Connections:** Surround yourself with a tribe that nurtures your growth. Genuine friends and a supportive community can strengthen your resolve to reclaim personal space.
3. **Establish Daily Rituals:** Design rituals exclusively for yourself. It could be savoring morning coffee in solitude or unwinding with a book in the evening. These daily practices become the rituals of self-love.
4. **Learn to Say No:** Reclaiming autonomy involves

mastering the art of saying "no." If the narcissist once dictated your choices, now you are the master of your life. Recognize your limits and assertively say no to anything that compromises your well-being.

5. **Professional Guidance:** Seeking therapy or counseling provides a structured path to rediscovering autonomy. A professional can guide you, offering insights and coping mechanisms tailored to your experience.

6. **Grey Rock Strategy:** The Grey Rock strategy involves becoming as uninteresting and unresponsive as a grey rock when dealing with the narcissist. Limit emotional reactions, avoid drama, and maintain a neutral demeanor. This strategy helps minimize their interest in manipulating or controlling you (Villines, 2023).

Escape the Chains: A Plan and Checklist to Break Free From a Narcissist

Leaving a relationship with a narcissist is a courageous step toward reclaiming your life, but it's a delicate dance requiring careful planning. The aftermath of such a decision can be challenging, as the narcissist, feeling a loss of control, may resort to post-separation abuse. Here's your roadmap to liberation, ensuring your safety and a smoother journey to autonomy (Krill, 2023):

Step 1: Safeguard All Living Beings

If you have dependents, ensure their safety. Plan for their needs, from shelter to legal considerations. Consult legal professionals for child custody matters and gather the necessary documentation for pets.

Step 2: Fortify Personal Belongings

Identify and protect crucial documents like passports, medical records, and legal paperwork. Safeguard sentimental items and titles that the narcissist might use against you.

Step 3: Unleash Cybersecurity Measures

Change passwords for email accounts, social media, and online banking. Erase digital traces of your connection with the narcissist, and refrain from posting about them on social media.

Step 4: Empower Your Finances

Change beneficiaries on financial accounts, revoke access to shared credit cards, and withdraw cash discreetly. Seek legal advice if financial entanglements are complex.

Step 5: Establish Emergency Protocols

Share your situation with trustworthy neighbors, create a code word with a friend for emergencies, and, if possible, install a security system.

Step 6: Assemble a Support System

Rebuild your social network, educating them about narcissism. Join survivor networks for additional support. Seek counseling to process emotions and consider legal advice.

Step 7: Channel Anger Into Empowerment

Acknowledge and manage anger constructively. Use it as fuel for positive change rather than allowing it to become a destructive force.

Step 8: Address Exhaustion

Prioritize self-care, including adequate rest. Retreat to a safe place if needed. Recognize that exhaustion is a byproduct of the narcissist's manipulation.

Step 9: Navigate the Legal Landscape

Seek legal counsel experienced in dealing with narcissistic personalities. Prepare for potential child custody battles and involve child protection services if necessary.

Step 10: Achieve Emotional Recovery

Set goals, limit grieving periods, and educate yourself on narcissistic tactics. Seek counseling to heal from the emotional trauma of the relationship.

BUILDING A RECOVERY TOOLBOX

Breaking free from the chains of a narcissistic relationship is a journey of healing, where the heart and mind often tread divergent paths. To facilitate this union, consider crafting a recovery toolbox—a collection of exercises and insights to bridge the gap between your emotional longing and the harsh reality (Greenberg, 2021).

Essential Tools for Healing

Building a recovery toolbox provides a practical framework for healing, helping you move beyond the emotional push-and-pull. Remember, it's not about forgetting but about acknowledging reality and empowering yourself for a future free from the chains of a toxic past.

Build Resilience

Building resilience is an art, not a trait, involving a nuanced process rooted in science-backed strategies. By incorporating resilience-building strategies into your life, you can fortify your inner strength, enabling you to bounce back from adversity and navigate life's ups and downs more effectively.

1. **Cultivate a Growth Mindset:** Embrace challenges as opportunities for growth rather than insurmountable obstacles. For example, view setbacks as your chance to develop new skills or growth strategies.

2. **Develop Social Connections:** Foster supportive relationships with friends, family, or colleagues. These connections provide emotional support during tough times. For instance, actively participate in social events or join clubs to expand your social network.

3. **Practice Self-Compassion:** Treat yourself with kindness and understanding, especially during challenging moments. For example, instead of harsh self-criticism after a mistake, acknowledge the experience as a chance to learn and improve.

4. **Maintain a Healthy Lifestyle:** Prioritize physical health through regular exercise, balanced nutrition, and sufficient sleep. A resilient body contributes to a resilient mind. An example would be incorporating a daily exercise routine or adopting mindful eating habits.

Reduce Stress

Embarking on a stress-busting journey doesn't require grand gestures; sometimes, it's about discovering the power within simple acts. Implementing a mix of quick stress busters for immediate relief and adopting longer-term strategies create a comprehensive approach to stress management. Following quick stress busters is incredibly effective in coping with stress (Fry & Dimitnu, 2022).

1. **Deep Breathing:** Inhale deeply for a count of four, hold for four, and exhale for four, then repeat.
2. **Stretch Breaks:** Stand up, stretch your arms overhead, and reach for your toes to release tension.
3. **Mindful Pause:** Take a few moments to focus on your senses, grounding yourself in the present.
4. **Laugh Therapy:** Watch a funny video or recall a humorous moment to lighten the mood.
5. **Quick Walk:** Take a 10-minute brisk walk to boost endorphins and reduce stress hormones.
6. **Positive Affirmations:** Repeat uplifting statements to counteract negative thoughts.

Adopting a holistic approach is crucial to managing stress effectively in the long run. Establishing a regular exercise routine, be it through jogging or yoga, can significantly contribute to stress reduction by promoting physical well-being. Mindfulness meditation in your daily practices provides sustained mental clarity and emotional balance. Engaging in hobbies like painting, gardening, or playing a musical instrument becomes a creative outlet for stress release.

Get Quality Sleep

Sleep is crucial for overall well-being, as it plays a vital role in physical health, cognitive function, and emotional balance. It allows the body to repair, regenerate, and consolidate memories. The amount of sleep needed varies by age, but adults generally require 7–9 hours.

During times of grief or trauma, the need for sleep often increases. Sleep aids in emotional regulation, memory processing, and coping mechanisms. Adequate sleep helps you navigate the challenges associated with grief and trauma, promoting resilience. Sleep promotes the release of growth hormones, repairs damaged cells, and strengthens neural connections. This healing process is vital for emotional well-being, especially during challenging times like grief or trauma.

Be Mindful

Mindfulness encompasses various techniques to cultivate present-moment awareness. Standard practices include meditation, deep breathing, body scanning, and mindful walking. These techniques aim to bring attention to the current experience without judgment. Incorporating mindfulness into your daily life means integrating it into your routine activities.

The following tips can help you infuse mindfulness into your life, fostering a more present and aware mindset (Paul et al., 2023):

1. **Start Small:** Begin with short sessions and gradually extend the duration.
2. **Consistency Matters:** Regular practice is the key; even brief daily sessions can yield benefits.
3. **Nonjudgmental Observation:** Approach thoughts and feelings with curiosity without labeling them as good or bad.
4. **App Integration:** Utilize mindfulness apps for guided sessions and tracking progress.
5. **Mindful Breathing:** Incorporate focused breathing exercises in moments of stress.
6. **Nature Connection:** Spend time outdoors, engaging your senses mindfully in natural surroundings.
7. **Mindful Eating:** Slow down, savor flavors, and focus on your eating actions.

Role of Self-Care and Self-Love in Personal Healing

Self-care practices form a customizable toolkit for healing and growth. As you cultivate these habits, you enhance your personal well-being and contribute positively to your community and the world. Drawing an analogy from the safety instructions on a flight, you need to secure your oxygen mask before assisting others—emphasizing the importance of self-nurturing. Once, Chidera Eggerue, a Skillshare instructor and activist, famously stated: "The world around me won't change until I do." Eggerue's words underscore the transformative power of self-care practices for personal benefit and for contributing positively to the world.

Following are some proven strategies for self-care and self-love:

1. **Journaling for Self-Discovery:** Initiate a journaling practice to delve into self-reflection, chart your growth, and release stressful thoughts.
2. **Intentional Rest:** Slow down deliberately in your daily life, dedicating moments to stillness and providing mental respite.
3. **Strengthen Connections:** Spend quality time with loved ones, nurturing essential relationships for overall wellness.
4. **Embrace Mantras:** Use affirming phrases to shape positive thoughts and reassure yourself during challenging moments.

Strategies for Emotional Regulation

Next time you find yourself in the whirlwind of emotions, remember that it's not about suppressing the waves but learning to navigate them like a seasoned sailor of your emotional seas. Let's break down the strategies for emotional regulation (Chowdhury, 2023).

Identify Emotions: Unveiling the Emotion Wheel

Have you ever felt lost in a sea of emotions? Now, you can identify your emotions using the emotional wheel as your compass. It's like Google Maps for your feelings, helping you pinpoint what you're experiencing. From joyous yellows to melancholic blues, the wheel categorizes emotions, guiding your understanding of the nuances of your feelings. You can find a typical emotional wheel in various mental health resources or apps; it's a game-changer in deciphering the intricate landscape of your emotional world.

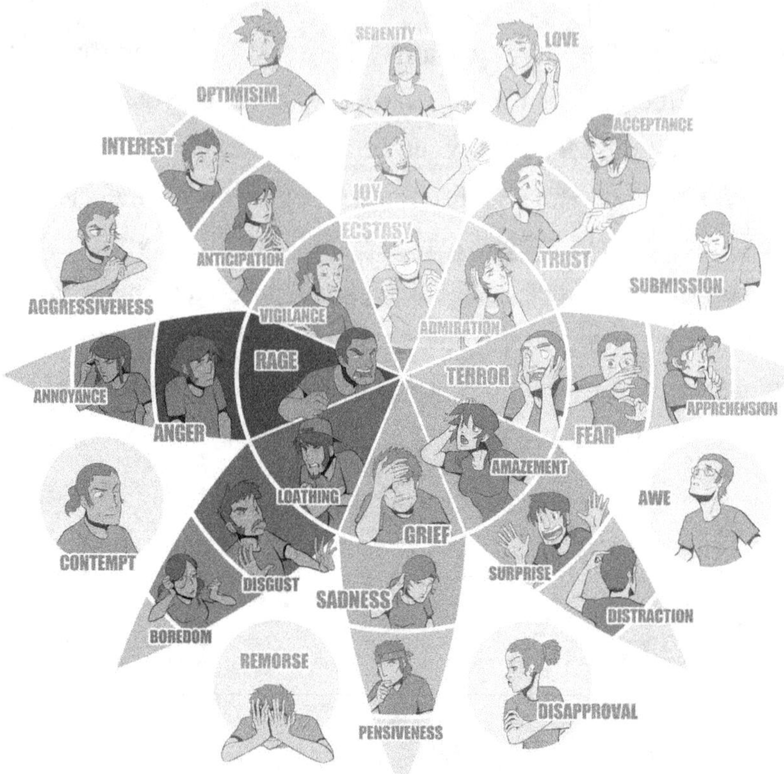

Figure 4. Robert Plutchik's emotional wheel (Wikimedia, Creative Commons)

Embrace Emotional Awareness

Building emotional awareness is similar to turning on the headlights in the dark tunnel of feelings. Understand what triggers specific emotions and acknowledge them without judgment. Each emotion has a story, whether it's the exhilaration of success or the sting of failure. Accepting and exploring these stories is vital to mastering the art of emotional regulation.

Channeling the Storm: From Destructive to Constructive

Have you ever been so angry that you could erupt like a volcano? Instead of letting emotions wreak havoc, channel them constructively. For instance, transform your anger into a workout, unleashing the fury through a training session. To cope with sadness, dive into creative expressions like painting or writing. By redirecting emotions into purposeful actions, you release pent-up energy and cultivate a healthier emotional landscape.

INTERACTIVE EXERCISE: DIVE INTO EMOTIONAL AWARENESS

Below are three powerful exercises that can transform how you understand and regulate your emotions. As you embark on this interactive experience, remember that it's all about self-discovery and growth. Let's dive in!

Exercise 1: Mindful Breathing

Skills: *Mindfulness, Self-Reflection, Self-Compassion*
Time: *5 minutes*

Mindful breathing is a practice that can revolutionize your emotional intelligence. Find a quiet spot, close your eyes, and focus on your breath. Inhale slowly, feeling the air fill your lungs, then exhale, letting go of the tension. Notice how your body responds. Can you commit to 5 minutes of this mindful breathing journey? Your emotional well-being is about to thank you.

Exercise 2: Journaling

Skills: *Self-Reflection, Self-Compassion, Empathy*
Time: *10–15 minutes*

Grab a journal and embark on a journey of self-reflection. Write freely about your thoughts and emotions without judgment. No need to worry about grammar or spelling; this is your personal space. Explore your inner world, notice patterns, and reflect on your writing. How do you feel after this 10–15-minute exploration? Any insights or revelations?

Exercise 3: Labeling Emotions

Skills: *Self-Compassion, Self-Reflection, Mindfulness*
Time: *10–20 minutes*

Dive into the ocean of your emotions. Take time to identify and label what you're feeling. Studies show that this simple act can reduce the intensity of negative emotions. Are you ready to spend 10–20 minutes on this exercise? It's an investment in understanding yourself on a deeper level. After all, knowing is the first step to managing.

Post-Exercise Questions

1. How long were you able to practice mindful breathing?

a) Less than 5 minutes

b) Around 5–10 minutes

c) More than 10 minutes

2. What insights did you gain from your journaling experience?

a) I discovered new aspects of my emotions.

b) It was a familiar journey with no significant insights.

c) I found the process challenging.

3. Did labeling your emotions impact the intensity of how you felt?

a) Yes, I felt a positive shift.

b) I didn't notice a significant change.

c) It made me more aware of my emotions.

Recovery isn't just about healing; it's also about creating a fortified future against further harm. Now, let's brace ourselves for setting unyielding boundaries to reclaim our lives!

CHAPTER 5
SETTING UNYIELDING BOUNDARIES

Setting emotional boundaries prevents people from manipulating you, using you, and playing with your feelings.

REMEZ SASSON

In the complex dance of life, imagine your soul as a house with various rooms, each holding the fragments of your identity. Imagine the doors of this house constantly swinging open, allowing unwelcome guests to wander freely. This metaphor encapsulates the essence of the importance of boundaries—those invisible but crucial lines that safeguard the sanctity of your inner abode. Just as a house needs doors to keep out unwanted intruders, your emotional well-being requires boundaries to shield you from manipulation, preserve your self-respect, and regain control. As we delve into this chapter, let's explore the philosophy of boundaries, understand their pivotal role in self-respect, and discern the fine line between walls that isolate and boundaries that empower them. Welcome to the realm where you become the architect of your emotional fortress.

THE PHILOSOPHY OF BOUNDARIES

Understanding the philosophy of boundaries reveals their significance in the intricate dance of relationships. They are not barriers to keep people out but rather gatekeepers that decide who gets a backstage pass to the concert of your life. This philosophy emphasizes that setting boundaries is not an act of exclusion but an embodiment of self-respect, a declaration that your emotional sanctuary deserves the utmost reverence.

IMPORTANCE OF BOUNDARIES

Imagine boundaries as the unspoken agreements that safeguard your emotional and physical sanctuaries. They aren't restrictions; they're the architects of healthy relationships, offering a blueprint for harmonious coexistence. Boundaries provide a sense of control over the delicate balance of time, space, and relationships. By cultivating the art of setting and maintaining boundaries, you embark on a journey toward independence and establish the foundation for nurturing positive connections with others (Better Help Editorial Team, 2023).

TYPES OF BOUNDARIES

Let's explore the seven types of boundaries that serve as the building blocks of this emotional fortress:

1. **Emotional Boundaries:** By shielding your feelings, emotional boundaries empower you to decide which personal information is open for discussion. "I'm not comfortable discussing that" becomes not just a phrase but a powerful boundary-setting mantra.

2. **Material Boundaries:** From personal belongings to living spaces, material boundaries establish the parameters of comfort regarding sharing and interaction. Your computer, your space—your rules.

3. **Intellectual Boundaries:** Thoughts and beliefs are personal territories. Intellectual boundaries dictate what you feel comfortable discussing, ensuring your views are respected and not dismissed.

4. **Physical Boundaries:** Concerned with personal space and physical contact, these boundaries allow you to define your comfort levels—whether it's hugging, standing close, or maintaining distance.

5. **Sexual Boundaries:** Crucial for consent and comfort, sexual boundaries draw clear lines on what is and isn't acceptable. "No" is not just a word; it's a boundary set in stone.

6. **Time Boundaries:** How you spend your time reflects your values. Time boundaries help align your activities

with your priorities, be it work-life balance, family time, or personal well-being.

THE BENEFITS OF HEALTHY BOUNDARIES

Setting and respecting boundaries isn't just a practice; it's a transformative journey with tangible benefits:

1. **Protecting Emotional Space:** Boundary-setting becomes a shield, preserving your emotional well-being and fostering self-respect and self-compassion.
2. **Protecting Physical Space:** Beyond personal comfort, physical boundaries extend to safeguarding possessions and the spaces you inhabit, allowing you to care for what's yours.
3. **Separating Thoughts, Feelings, and Needs:** Healthy boundaries prevent emotional exhaustion by distinguishing between your responsibilities and those of others.
4. **Enriching Relationships:** Strong boundaries pave the way for healthier connections, freeing you from resentment and insecurity.
5. **Protecting Valuable Time:** Time, once spent, can't be reclaimed. Boundaries ensure that your time is spent on what truly matters to you.
6. **Having a Strong Sense of Identity:** Boundaries are the compass guiding you back to yourself, ensuring your identity, goals, and needs are never compromised.

Setting Boundaries as Acts of Self-Respect: Reclaiming Your Power

Contrary to the fear that setting boundaries might transform you into an unapproachable figure, the reality is empowering. Establishing clear guidelines for how you wish to be treated not only commands respect but also contributes to the overall improvement of relationships (Neal, 2021). While it may take time for others to adjust, consistency in upholding boundaries fosters adaptation. The alternative—enduring mistreatment silently—corrodes relationships over time. Setting boundaries becomes an assertion of your needs, creating a space where your well-being and happiness can flourish.

Navigating Between Walls and Boundaries: A Tale of Liberation

Walls are rigid defenses born out of survival, limiting personal growth and isolating individuals from genuine connections. They are reactive measures that, while initially protective, can lead to exhaustion and emotional detachment. In contrast, boundaries are personal guidelines, an expression of self-love that dictates how one expects to be treated. Unlike walls, boundaries are not defensive walls; instead, they are affirmations of personal values and limits (Moore, 2021).

Kim Moore, the founder of Blossome Support Network, shares her journey of self-discovery while highlighting the subtle distinction between walls and boundaries. In the face of her husband's alcoholism, she initially erected walls as a protective measure, seeking refuge from the chaos. However, these walls, while instinctual, inadvertently isolated her from crucial, healthy connections. Through therapy, Kim discerned the crucial disparity. Walls, reactive defenses rooted in survival restricted personal growth and led to emotional detachment. In contrast, boundaries emerged as self-loving guidelines, shaping how she expected to be treated. Her decision to leave her husband became a transformative act of boundary-setting, signaling a refusal to endure an unhealthy situation any longer (Moore, 2021).

IMPLEMENTING BOUNDARIES

Setting boundaries isn't just a theoretical concept; it's a transformative practice that reshapes the landscape of your relationships. Imagine it as the art of crafting a protective shield, allowing you to navigate the complexities of life with grace and self-respect. The first step is self-reflection—taking stock of your existing boundaries and discerning where you might need to draw clearer lines. For instance, consider how you feel after interactions with certain individuals. If exhaustion, guilt, or resentment lingers, it's a cue that your boundaries might need reinforcing.

Mastering the Art of Boundary Communication: Practical Tips for Success

Effective communication of boundaries is a nuanced skill, combining assertiveness and sensitivity. Implementing these practical tips will pave the way for effective boundary communication, fostering healthier relationships while safeguarding your mental well-being (Dalla-Camina, 2021). Here are practical ways to master this art:

Be Clear and Specific

When establishing boundaries, clarity is your ally. Avoid ambiguity by explicitly expressing your comfort zone and limitations. Instead of a vague "I don't like it when you're always late," opt for a direct and assertive approach: "I need you to be on time for our meetings." This precision leaves little room for misunderstanding.

Choose the Right Time and Place

Timing is crucial in boundary conversations. Choose a calm, private setting to discuss boundaries. Avoid addressing them during conflicts or heated moments. Ensure both parties are receptive, fostering an environment conducive to open and honest dialogue.

Use "I" Statements

Craft your boundaries using "I" statements, focusing on expressing your feelings and needs without sounding accusatory. Shift from "You always interrupt me" to "I feel frustrated when I am interrupted." This approach encourages understanding and open communication.

Set Consequences

Clearly articulate the repercussions of crossing boundaries. Communicate which actions are unacceptable and the potential outcomes if those boundaries are violated. For instance, if consistent disrespect occurs, convey the possibility of limiting or ending contact. This reinforces the importance of respecting established boundaries.

Active Listening

In boundary discussions, practice active listening. Encourage an open dialogue by understanding the other person's perspective and being willing to compromise when appropriate. Active listening involves giving full attention, summarizing the other person's points, and asking clarifying questions for a more meaningful exchange.

Be Consistent

Consistency is the linchpin of maintaining boundaries. Uphold them firmly and consistently to establish clear expectations over time. Sticking to your boundaries reinforces their importance and fosters respect, even in challenging or uncomfortable situations.

Navigating Boundary Ruptures: Strategies for Restoration

Boundaries, those invisible guardians of our well-being, can face breaches that lead to emotional, psychological, and even physical consequences. A boundary rupture occurs when others disregard our limits, infiltrating our personal space, emotions, time, or autonomy. These breaches vary from physical intrusion to emotional manipulation, profoundly affecting our well-being in personal, work, or social contexts (Klinzing, 2023).

Consequences of Boundary Ruptures

Boundary breaches yield diverse consequences, from emotional distress to physical harm. Long-term relationships may desensitize individuals to frequent violations, complicating the recognition of signs and consequences. Emotional distress, strained relationships, loss of autonomy, physical harm, diminished self-worth, codependency, and isolation are potential outcomes, depending on severity and frequency.

Strategies for Coping and Healing

Let's discuss some practical coping strategies for boundary rupture.

1. **Understand Your Own Boundaries:** Establish a clear understanding of your personal boundaries, reflecting on values and needs. Define comfort zones for each relationship context, differentiating between personal and professional boundaries.

2. **Validate Your Feelings:** Recognize and validate emotions arising from boundary ruptures without judgment. Allow time and space for feeling and processing these emotions, acknowledging discomfort as a natural part of the healing process.

3. **Practice Boundary Strengthening Techniques:** Use visualization techniques to reinforce personal boundaries. The "Filling the Space" visualization involves envisioning a protective bubble filled with a chosen color, preventing breaches unless permitted.

4. **Assertive Communication:** Clearly express boundaries

using assertive communication. State expectations firmly without over-explaining, remembering that "No" is a complete sentence. Avoid expecting others to understand your boundaries intuitively.

5. **Seek Support:** Engage friends, family, or professionals for support, gaining perspectives, validation, and guidance. Utilize your support network to navigate challenges associated with boundary ruptures.

Survivor Stories: Empowering Boundary-Setting

Survivor stories emphasize the diverse contexts in which individuals successfully implement boundary-setting strategies. From workplace challenges to familial dynamics and personal relationships, these narratives showcase the resilience and empowerment that emerge when individuals prioritize their well-being through effective boundary-setting.

Laura's Triumph Over Workplace Boundaries

Laura, a marketing professional, endured a persistent overload of tasks beyond the scope of her job description. Fearful of disappointing her superiors, she hesitated to set boundaries. Eventually, she mustered the courage to express her workload concerns. Surprisingly, her supervisors respected her honesty and adjusted her expectations. Laura's story showcases the transformative power of communicating boundaries, even in professional settings.

James's Healing Journey in a Toxic Friendship

James faced a draining friendship where his emotional well-being took a backseat. As he realized the toxic dynamics, he decided to set clear boundaries. Communicating openly about his needs and emotional limits, James distanced himself from the negativity. The result was a newfound sense of autonomy, emphasizing how boundary-setting can rejuvenate personal relationships.

Emma's Empowerment in Family Dynamics

Growing up with loose family boundaries, Emma habitually prioritized others' needs. Recognizing the toll on her mental health, she embarked on a journey to set boundaries with her family. Initially met with resistance, Emma persisted. Over time, her family adapted, leading to healthier relationships. Emma's story illustrates the transformative impact of asserting boundaries, even in long-standing familial connections.

David's Resilience Amid Workplace Pressure

David found himself consistently working overtime due to an unspoken office culture. As stress mounted, he decided to communicate his need for a healthier work-life balance. Initially met with skepticism, David's persistence led to a positive shift. Colleagues began respecting his boundaries, fostering a more sustainable and supportive work environment. David's experience highlights the importance of advocating for personal well-being in professional settings.

MAINTAINING AND ENFORCING BOUNDARIES: A PERSONAL TRIUMPH

Imagine your boundaries as the sturdy walls of a castle, delineating your emotional and physical territory. When respected, these walls create a haven, fostering positive mental health and robust relationships. However, when breached, consequences akin to an attack on the castle unfold, ranging from emotional distress to strained relationships and even physical harm. To strengthen your well-being fortress, understand its layout and define your emotional limits and values (Furlan & Schneider, 2022).

How to Set Boundaries if You Are Scared to Do So

Setting boundaries can be intimidating, especially if fear of conflict or rejection looms large. Begin by clearly identifying what you need and understanding that establishing boundaries is fundamental to self-care. Start small, communicating limits in less challenging situations first, and gradually work your way up to more complex scenarios.

How to Say No – Especially at First

Saying no, mainly when you're not accustomed to it, requires practice and a shift in mindset. Understand that saying no is not a rejection of others but a prioritization of your own needs. Be firm and concise in your response, avoiding unnecessary explanations that may weaken your stance. It's essential to recognize that saying no is a skill that improves with repetition. Start with low-stakes situations, and as you become more comfortable, you'll find it easier to assert your boundaries in more challenging circumstances.

How to Not Feel Bad About Your Boundaries

Avoiding the guilt or discomfort associated with setting boundaries requires a shift in perspective. Remind yourself that establishing and maintaining boundaries is crucial for your well-being and does not make you selfish. Recognize that it's natural for others to have different needs and reactions, and that's okay. Practice self-affirmation, focusing on the positive impact of your boundaries on your mental health and relationships. Surround yourself with a supportive network that understands and respects the importance of personal limits, reinforcing your confidence in upholding and enforcing boundaries.

Consistency Is Key

Consistency is paramount in maintaining boundaries across various relationships. In family dynamics, setting consistent expectations on privacy or communication helps establish a respectful environment. In parenting, maintaining consistent rules reinforces a child's understanding of limits and fosters a secure upbringing. In couples, consistency in respecting each other's personal space and emotional needs builds a foundation of trust. In the workplace, consistently reinforcing professional boundaries ensures a healthy and respectful work environment. Whether familial, parental, romantic, or professional, upholding consistent boundaries is fundamental for nurturing respectful and thriving relationships.

Handling Boundary Violations: Top 5 Steps You Can Take

Handling boundary violations requires a strategic approach to maintaining your personal space. Taking radical steps to hold onto boundaries is a journey that requires commitment and self-compassion (Casabianca, 2022).

1. **Clarify Your Boundaries:** Setting boundaries is vital, but clarity is key. Clearly define where you draw the line in specific situations. For example, instead of a vague boundary like "I won't lend money if borrowed too much," specify, "I am willing to lend up to $1,000, expecting repayment within three months. Failure to do so means no further loans."

2. **Communicate Your Boundaries Directly:** Sugarcoating boundaries to avoid discomfort leads to constant violations. Clearly express your boundaries without overexplanation. For instance, say, "I prefer not to discuss personal matters," or "Please avoid calling me at X time without asking why."

3. **Establish Clear Consequences of Boundary Violation:** Set realistic and clear consequences for boundary violations. For instance, "If you make unwelcome advances, I will leave." Clear repercussions enhance the effectiveness of your boundaries.

4. **Stay Consistent:** Consistency is crucial. Enforce your boundaries consistently; otherwise, people may cross them at will. Whether with family, friends, or colleagues, consistently following through on set boundaries establishes their credibility.

5. **Maintain Your Stand, Especially During Resistance:** Expect resistance, but stand firm. Calmly remind others of your boundaries and reinforce that you won't compromise. For instance, say, "I appreciate your feelings, but I need you to respect my boundaries. I won't meet if my personal space isn't respected."

Reinforcement Techniques

Reinforcing personal boundaries through assertiveness techniques is crucial for maintaining self-worth and cultivating healthy relationships (Minor, 2020). Here are six effective techniques:

1. **Broken Record Technique:** Challenge the belief that your response should depend on what others say first. Calmly repeat your message without getting sidetracked, emphasizing your commitment until the desired result is achieved.

2. **Fogging or Clouding:** When faced with negative criticism, create psychological distance by acknowledging the critic's frustration without directly responding to the negative implications. This sets up

clear boundary lines and reduces the frequency of criticism.

3. **Negative Inquiry:** With people close to you, distinguish between truthful feedback and manipulative judgments. Prompt further criticism or information about alleged wrongdoing in an unemotional manner to break the manipulative cycle.

4. **Negative Assertion:** Acknowledge your mistakes without justification or defense. This promotes self-acceptance, minimizes hostility, and prevents escalation of emotions.

5. **Putting the Ball Back in Their Court:** Effectively deflect inappropriate questions by posing questions in return, such as "Why do you need to know?" or "Why would you ask such a question?"

6. **Asserting Your Right Not to Answer the Question:** Clearly state your discomfort in responding to a particular question, reinforcing your right to maintain privacy.

BOUNDARY REFLECTION TOOL

Take a moment to reflect on various aspects of your life and assess if your boundaries are being respected or if there are areas where they might be crossed. After identifying such areas, consider possible actions you can take to reinforce your boundaries.

Personal Space

- Reflect on your personal space, both physically and emotionally.
- Have there been instances where someone invaded your physical space without consent?
- Has someone made you uncomfortable by prying into your personal emotions?

Action Steps:

- Set clear physical boundaries and communicate them assertively.
- Politely but firmly express when a topic is too personal and you prefer not to discuss it.

Time Management

- Evaluate how your time is being utilized and if others respect your schedule.
- Do you find yourself constantly overwhelmed with commitments due to difficulty saying no?

Action Steps:

- Learn to say no when necessary without overexplaining.
- Prioritize your time and communicate your availability clearly.

Workplace Boundaries

- Consider your professional environment.
- Are colleagues or superiors making demands that infringe on your personal time?
- Do you feel pressured to take on tasks beyond the scope of your job description?

Action Steps:

- Establish clear boundaries regarding your work hours and responsibilities.
- Politely but assertively decline tasks that fall outside your role.

Digital Boundaries

- Reflect on your online interactions.
- Are there individuals who consistently overstep your digital boundaries?
- Do you find it challenging to disconnect from your devices?

Action Steps:

- Set specific times for digital detox and communicate this to those around you.
- Use privacy settings to control who has access to your personal information.

Social Relationships

- Assess your interactions with friends and family.
- Are there relationships causing emotional distress or draining your energy?
- Have you clearly communicated your needs in these relationships?

Action Steps:

- Identify and communicate your emotional limits in relationships.
- Seek support from friends or professionals when needed.

Self-Care

- Consider your personal well-being.
- Do you often neglect self-care due to external demands?
- Are there activities or situations that consistently leave you feeling drained?

Action Steps:

- Prioritize self-care activities and allocate time for them regularly.
- Communicate your need for personal time and self-care to those close to you.

Reflections and Action Plans

Areas where boundaries are crossed:

- Personal Space: _________
- Time Management: _________
- Workplace Boundaries: _________
- Digital Boundaries: _
- Social Relationships: _________
- Self-Care: _________

Actions I can take:

- Personal Space: _________
- Time Management: _________
- Workplace Boundaries: _________
- Digital Boundaries: _
- Social Relationships: _________
- Self-Care: _________

Remember, setting and reinforcing boundaries is a continuous process. Regularly revisit and adjust your boundaries as needed. Your well-being is a priority! In the next chapter, we move on to explore the stages of healing by examining self-worth.

Make a Difference with Your Review
The Narcissistic Abuse Recovery Blueprint

Unlock the Power of Generosity

"In the aftermath of narcissistic abuse, every act of kindness we extend to others plants a seed of healing in both their heart and ours, blossoming into a shared sanctuary of recovery and hope."
Did you know that when we do nice things for others without expecting anything back, it can make us feel really worthwhile? It's like when you share your favorite snack with a friend, and it makes you both happy. That's the magic of being generous!
So, I've got a special question for you...
Would you be willing to help out a friend you haven't met yet, even if they might not be able to say thank you?
Think about someone who's feeling really mixed up and hurt inside because of the way someone else has treated them. Maybe they're feeling a lot like you did before. They're looking for a little bit of light in a pretty dark place, but they're not sure where to find it.
I want to help everyone feel better and find their way out of that dark place. Everything I do is about helping more and more people. But I need your help to reach as many people as we can.
That's where you come in! Believe it or not, what you think about this book can really help. When you tell others how this book helped you, it's like you're holding out a flashlight in the dark for them to see by.
So, on behalf of a friend out there who's still looking for that light, could you take a minute to share how this book helped you?
It doesn't cost anything but a little bit of your time, and it could really make a big difference for someone else. Your words might help...

...another kid feel less alone.
...another family start to heal.
...another heart to find courage.
...another person to take that first step.

...another story to have a happy beginning.
To spread some kindness and hope into someone's world, all you need to do is share your thoughts about this book. It's super easy and quick! Just scan the QR code below to leave your review:

Scan here!

If the idea of helping someone out there makes you smile, then you're exactly the kind of friend we're looking for. Welcome to the circle of kindness!

I'm so excited to be on this journey with you. The tips and ideas we're going to explore together are going to help you so much.

Thank you from the very bottom of my heart. Now, let's jump back into our adventure of healing and growing stronger together.

Your friend and guide,

K. C. Mallette

P.S. - Remember, sharing a little bit of kindness can make a big difference. If this book has helped you, and you think it could help someone else, why not pass it along?

CHAPTER 6

REDISCOVERING SELF-WORTH

Have you been in a crowded room but felt like you were alone? Have you ever felt like a puzzle with missing pieces? Have you always been that shoulder to cry on? Have you felt so empty that the darkness takes over?

UNKNOWN

Amid the clamor of a bustling room, Maria often felt like a muted whisper eclipsed by vibrant conversations. The vivid hues of laughter and connection painted a sharp contrast to her eroded self-worth, rendering her a phantom in a sea of vibrant souls. Even though Maria was physically close, she was overshadowed by lively conversations that ignored her. In these moments, she felt the pain of being invisible. Her attempts to connect were ignored, making her feel even lonelier. It was in these moments that she realized that her past relationship isolated her from the world, both physically and emotionally.

THE EROSION OF SELF-WORTH

While navigating the tumultuous aftermath of an abusive relationship, the erosion of self-worth becomes a haunting companion. Imagine standing on shifting sands, the ground beneath you constantly giving way, leaving you unsteady and unsure. In the insidious dance with a narcissist, the very fabric of confidence unravels. They wield manipulation like a chisel, carving away self-esteem and leaving behind a sculpture of doubt. Every cruel word and every belittling remark etch a mark on the canvas of self-worth. It's a slow, silent erosion where the victim becomes a mere echo of their former self, haunted by the echoes of an internalized abuser. The signs are subtle yet profound—a hesitant voice, averted eyes, and a spirit withering under the weight of relentless criticism. The erosion of self-worth is a silent thief that steals joy, leaving behind a hollow silhouette yearning to be whole again.

HOW NARCISSISTS SYSTEMATICALLY ERODE SELF-WORTH?

The intricate art of narcissistic erosion unfolds through a carefully curated arsenal of phrases and tactics. Imagine navigating a verbal minefield where every word is a strategic move designed to chip away at your self-worth. The narcissist employs phrases like "you're too sensitive" or "I hate drama" as psychological weapons, leaving you questioning your own perceptions. They master the subtle snipe, casting negativity like a silent assassin, and seamlessly shift blame to preserve their ego, leaving you bewildered and doubting your actions (Waller, 2018).

Creating confrontation is their playground, a twisted arena where they bask in false superiority, and they are not afraid to bend the truth, insisting you are wrong until you question your own reality. The narcissist is a puppeteer, pulling strings to gain allies and weaving a web that traps you in self-doubt. With a Jekyll and Hyde personality, they charm and manipulate, leaving you hooked until the mask slips, revealing the calculated nature of their psychological warfare.

THE INTERNALIZED VOICE OF THE ABUSER

The internalized voice of the abuser, a haunting echo within the corridors of the mind, manifests itself as a relentless critic wielding the weapons of manipulation. Imagine a sinister whisper convincing you that you are never enough, a constant companion eroding your self-worth (Damascan, 2021). This internal saboteur mimics the abuser's phrases, replaying demeaning remarks like a broken record. "You are worthless" becomes a cruel mantra, echoing in moments of vulnerability. Picture a distorted mirror reflecting an altered reality, where the abuser's judgments embed themselves as your own. The internalized voice doesn't just criticize; it distorts perceptions, making you question your every move. It's a captive audience to the abuser's script—a captive audience you must break free from to reclaim your narrative.

EMOTIONAL RAMIFICATIONS OF LOST SELF-ESTEEM

The emotional aftermath of lost self-esteem is a turbulent landscape where shadows of doubt are long and dark. Imagine a once vibrant garden, now overgrown with the weeds of insecurity. Every setback feels like a confirmation of inadequacy, a heavy burden on shoulders that once stood tall. Anxiety becomes your constant companion, whispering worst-case scenarios and feeding on the fragments of self-doubt. In this emotional realm, the most straightforward tasks transform into daunting challenges, and the pursuit of happiness feels like a distant dream. Restoring self-esteem becomes not just a goal but a vital journey toward reclaiming your emotional well-being.

Signs of Low Self Esteem

Navigating life with low self-esteem is like walking through a fog where doubts and insecurities lurk in every shadow. This struggle manifests in various ways, from an aversion to asking for help to a perpetual dance with worry and doubt. Compliments become a source of discomfort, like a foreign language they can't quite comprehend. The future appears through a pessimistic lens, and establishing boundaries becomes daunting. It is a landscape where being a people-pleaser is both a coping mechanism and a silent plea for validation. Recognizing and addressing these signs becomes a crucial step in the journey toward rebuilding self-esteem and reclaiming a positive outlook on life (Cherry, 2023).

Correction of Self-Esteem Through Emotional Resilience

Building emotional resilience is akin to constructing a sturdy bridge between self-esteem and life's challenges. Imagine self-esteem as the bedrock, the unshakeable "I am" foundation that forms the core of our being. Contrast it with confidence, the "I can" aspect that deals with our capabilities. While confidence can be a facade, a quick fix through the "fake it until you make it" mantra, self-esteem, on the other hand, is a profound and enduring reservoir.

Picture someone who exudes confidence, strutting through life's challenges, only to crumble when faced with a single event that exceeds their capabilities. On the other hand, a person with a healthy sense of self-esteem possesses the resilience to rebuild shattered confidence. It's the understanding that, no matter what happens, they will always be okay. Recognizing and nurturing this foundational "I am" perspective becomes pivotal in navigating stress, regulating emotions, and ultimately fostering emotional resilience (Hall, 2016).

REBUILDING A POSITIVE SELF-IMAGE

Building a positive self-image is a transformative journey that involves revisiting the carefree days of childhood, embracing gratitude, and actively participating in the growth process. Think back to when you were a child, unburdened by the judgments of others. Embrace the playfulness, the willingness to try new things, and the ability to laugh at yourself.

The Power of Affirmations

Positive affirmations are powerful tools for transforming negative thoughts into positive ones, fostering a positive mental attitude, and improving mental fitness. They work by creating new neural pathways in the brain through the process of neuroplasticity. By repeating positive statements regularly, these affirmations become part of the brain's physical structure, leading to more positive automatic thoughts.

Benefits of Positive Affirmations

Let's discuss some of the notable benefits of positive affirmations (Perry, 2022).

1. **Decrease Negative Self-Talk:** Affirmations help reduce negative self-talk, promoting a healthier internal dialogue.
2. **Increase Positive Thinking:** Positive affirmations contribute to a more optimistic mindset, influencing beliefs and behaviors over time.
3. **Enhance Self-Worth:** Using affirmations aids in improving self-worth, cultivating a positive self-image, and boosting self-confidence.
4. **Improve Mental and Physical Health:** Positive daily affirmations can positively impact mental health, fitness, and even physical well-being.
5. **Strengthen Problem-Solving Abilities:** Affirmations contribute to developing a mindset that is resilient in the face of challenges and enhances problem-solving skills.

Top 10 Positive Affirmations

Incorporating the following affirmations into daily practice can contribute to positive self-transformation, reshaping thought patterns and beliefs over time.

1. **I am enough. I have enough** – Boosts confidence and counters feelings of inadequacy or self-doubt, fostering an abundance mindset.

2. **I am in the right place, at the right time, doing the right thing** – Helps combat comparison and aligns with your path, freeing you from societal expectations.

3. **I can do hard things** – Provides encouragement when facing overwhelming challenges, fostering resilience.

4. **I allow myself to be more fully me** – Encourages self-acceptance and authenticity, allowing you to embrace your true self.

5. **I believe in myself** – Cultivates self-belief, providing the courage to tackle challenges, even in the face of doubt.

6. **I am grateful for another day of life** – Promotes gratitude, helping you live life more fully and appreciate each moment.

7. **I am worthy of what I desire** – Empowers you to pursue dreams and passions without self-imposed limitations.

8. **I choose myself** – Grants permission to prioritize personal goals and desires without waiting for external validation.

9. **I am resilient in the face of challenges** – Affirms your

strength and resilience, reinforcing the ability to overcome obstacles.

10. **I am proud of myself and my achievements** – Encourages self-appreciation, detaching from comparison and external validations.

The Role of Therapy and Self-Reflection

While therapy provides professional guidance, integrating self-reflection into daily life empowers individuals to take control of their emotional well-being, break unproductive patterns, and navigate the journey to self-discovery with resilience and authenticity. Learning the art of reflection involves a deliberate and conscious effort to understand our thoughts, feelings, motivations, reactions, and responses. By gaining a more honest perspective on our behaviors, we can identify emotional blind spots and stay focused on our goals, ultimately achieving greater satisfaction in life (Rice, 2017).

The process of reflection is accessible to everyone, with many familiar with the basics of pondering past events, considering alternative scenarios, or contemplating pivotal decisions. Some may choose to maintain a journal, while others prefer allowing their minds to wander freely on a specific topic. Regardless of the method, bringing structure to reflection is vital.

You can embark on a self-reflection journey by using the following strategies:

1. **Focus on a Recent Event:** Delve into an event that didn't go as planned.
2. **Hold Up a Mirror to Yourself:** Reflect without external influences, focusing solely on your perspective.
3. **Be Honest:** Commit to honesty about yourself, acknowledging both strengths and flaws.
4. **Be Courageous:** Authentic self-reflection requires courage to confront and consider personal flaws.
5. **Trust Your Instincts:** Recognize when insights resonate with you, trusting your judgment in the reflection process.

Celebrating Small Victories

Celebrating small victories is like sprinkling magic on the path to rebuilding a positive self-image. In the grand tapestry of personal growth, these small wins are the vibrant threads that weave a narrative of resilience and progress.

Gratitude becomes the mighty tool in this celebration arsenal. Imagine yourself deciding to overcome a fear or complete an impossible task. The moment you conquer it, no matter how seemingly insignificant, becomes a cause for celebration. Instead of downplaying these triumphs, gratitude steps in as the maestro, orchestrating a symphony of positive emotions.

For instance, imagine tackling a social situation that once sent shivers down your spine. As you navigate it successfully, express gratitude for the courage summoned and the personal growth achieved. Embrace the joy of overcoming, and let gratitude be your anthem. It transforms these seemingly small victories into milestones of self-discovery and empowerment. This celebration ritual is not about grandiosity but about acknowledging the incremental steps that lead to profound change.

NARRATIVES OF TRANSFORMATION

In the labyrinth of rediscovering self-worth after enduring narcissistic abuse, narratives of transformation emerge as guiding constellations. These are tales of resilience, whispered by those who have weathered the storms of manipulation and emerged from the shadows of self-doubt. Picture the protagonist, once entangled in the web of gaslighting, now glowing with empowerment. These narratives aren't merely stories but beacons of hope, illuminating the path for others to reclaim their worth.

Inspiring Stories of Survivors Reclaiming Their Worth

In the shadows of a seemingly idyllic mother-daughter relationship, Emily bore the weight of relentless criticism and emotional control. Her mother, a covert narcissist, expertly wielded belittling phrases and perpetual blame, leaving Emily feeling like an echo of herself. The epiphany struck when a close friend, recognizing the signs of abuse, gently encouraged Emily to confront the toxic dynamics. With the guidance of a therapist, Emily embarked on a journey of self-discovery. She dissected the layers of gaslighting that had obscured her true essence. In this crucible of healing, Emily reclaimed her worth and forged an unshakeable self-love that transcended the echoes of maternal manipulation.

In another narcissistic world, David faced a constant barrage of snide comments and blame-shifting from his siblings. The emotional toll was profound as he struggled to assert his identity in the suffocating shadow of his narcissistic brother. The pivotal moment materialized when a colleague, sensing David's silent suffering, recommended professional counseling. David confronted the deeply ingrained narratives of unworthiness as the therapeutic process unfolded. Setting boundaries became a potent tool, and with each fortified boundary, David reclaimed a fragment of his self-esteem. Celebrating these small victories, David dismantled the power dynamics that had long dictated his worth. His narrative stands as a testament to the transformative power embedded in resilience and self-assertion.

Navigating From Self-Doubt to Self-Assuredness

Embarking on your career or relationship journey often stirs the lurking specter of self-doubt, threatening to eclipse your potential. However, in this internal tussle, summoning your alter ego proves potent—not to adopt a new identity but to embrace a mindset propelling you beyond self-imposed limits. A study in Sage Journal reinforces this, highlighting that embodying a confident alter ego enhances resilience and assertiveness. Additionally, reshaping self-perception through others' eyes unveils overlooked strengths. Treating feedback as an art, discerning gems amid the noise, becomes paramount. Lastly, rewriting your internal script, validated by psychological research, works transformative wonders. As you waltz from doubt to assurance, these strategies, supported by empirical findings, light the way to your professional zenith.

Re-establishing a Connection With Oneself

Embarking on the tumultuous journey of daily life often leads us away from our authentic selves. Stress and frustration become unwelcome companions in pursuing external validation and societal conformity. However, the essence of a fulfilling life lies in reconnecting with our true selves. This isn't a mere suggestion; it's an imperative. According to Tony Robbins, there are six impactful ways to achieve this vital reconnection (Robins, 2023):

Discover Your Purpose

Unveiling your purpose is a transformative journey, allowing you to celebrate your unique gifts and understand your driving forces. Reflect on moments that bring you pure joy, and identify activities that make you feel alive when no one is watching—therein lies your purpose.

Understand and Meet Your Needs

Connecting with yourself is intricately tied to the Six Human Needs. Recognize your dominant need—be it certainty, significance, variety, love/connection, growth, or contribution. Fulfilling these needs is crucial for a fulfilled life.

Find Your Voice

Our authentic voice often gets muted by societal expectations. Use the power of song to reconnect with your unfiltered, authentic self. Sing along to your favorite tunes, or learn an instrument to awaken your true essence.

Reconnect With Yourself Physically

Dance becomes a gateway to self-expression and self-actualization, especially through practices like the 5 Rhythms. Embrace the power of movement to release the heart, free the mind, and connect with the soul's essence.

Start a Journal

Similar to music and dance, writing plays a role in self-connection. Journaling about experiences and emotions helps identify and accept feelings, clarify opinions, and strengthen ideas. It is a tool for self-discovery and mindset transformation.

Ask the Right Questions

The quality of your life is intertwined with the questions you ask yourself. Shift from disempowering inquiries to positive ones, focusing on gratitude, happiness, and commitment. This redirection of mental focus fosters a deeper connection with your true self.

PERSONAL STRENGTHS ANALYSIS TOOL

Instructions: Reflect on each statement and mark YES/NO based on your honest assessment of yourself.

Remember, this analysis is a tool for self-reflection and growth. Be honest with yourself, and use it to guide your journey to rediscover and affirm your self-worth.

1. **I am capable of setting healthy boundaries.** YES/NO
2. **I prioritize my well-being, including physical and mental health.** YES/NO
3. **I have a clear sense of my values and live in alignment with them.** YES/NO
4. **I can identify and express my needs in relationships.** YES/NO
5. **I am able to forgive myself for past mistakes and learn from them.** YES/NO
6. **I have a strong support system of friends and/or family.** YES/NO
7. **I engage in activities that bring me joy and fulfillment.** YES/NO
8. **I can differentiate between healthy and toxic relationships.** YES/NO
9. **I am able to assert myself respectfully in various situations.** YES/NO
10. **I celebrate my achievements and acknowledge my progress.** YES/NO
11. **I cultivate a positive self-image and avoid self-criticism.** YES/NO

CHAPTER 7
RECLAIMING RELATIONSHIPS AND TRUST

We need people in our lives with whom we can be as open as possible. To have real conversations with people may seem like such a simple, obvious suggestion, but it involves courage and risk.

THOMAS MOORE

As Sarah tentatively opened up to her best friend, Emily, about her struggles with trust after enduring narcissistic abuse, her voice trembled with vulnerability. She shared how the constant manipulation and deceit had left her second-guessing everyone's intentions, even those closest to her. With a reassuring smile, Emily reminded her of their enduring friendship and affirmed that, though wounded, trust could be rebuilt. She recounted instances of her strength and resilience, emphasizing how those who truly cared would stand by her side. Emily's encouraging words became a beacon of hope, urging Sarah to navigate the path of healing and gradually let trust bloom once more.

TRUST DILEMMA

Surviving narcissistic abuse is a journey fraught with profound challenges, and one enduring scar left in its wake is the shattering of trust. Victims, having been manipulated, gaslighted, and betrayed, find the very foundation of their trust eroded. Trust issues become the unwelcome companions of those who have braved narcissistic storms, casting shadows on the path to rebuilding connections.

How Narcissists Exploit and Erode Trust

Narcissists excel in the art of exploitation, weaving a web of deceit to entrap you. They consistently undermine your self-worth, creating a dependency that distorts your perception of trust. They plant seeds of doubt through calculated gaslighting, making you question your reality. The narcissist's charm, initially a beacon of trust, became a weapon of emotional destruction. This insidious erosion of trust is their modus operandi, leaving you grappling with the aftermath of shattered confidence and fractured belief in the authenticity of others (Shaw, 2023).

The Challenge of Trust Issues Post-Abuse

The aftermath of an abusive relationship leaves survivors grappling with the daunting challenge of rebuilding trust. The scars of betrayal and violations of safety linger, casting a shadow on the path to forming new connections (Gillis, 2023). Learning to trust again involves unlearning survival behaviors developed in the toxic past. Many survivors, having experienced family-of-origin trauma, may find themselves unconsciously drawn to replicating patterns, perpetuating cycles of pain. Recognizing red flags and setting boundaries becomes a crucial aspect of breaking free from the shackles of normalized abuse.

Navigating Relationships With Heightened Skepticism

Navigating relationships after narcissistic abuse often comes with the baggage of heightened skepticism, an armor born from past betrayal. This skepticism, while a double-edged sword, can serve as a tool for critical thinking and objective evaluation. The emotional scars of abuse reside on the right side of the brain, urging a need for balance with the skepticism rooted in the left side. Skepticism becomes problematic when emotional distancing occurs, forming a brick wall of doubt and suspicion. Partners find themselves questioning positive intentions, creating a chilly distance. Therefore, balancing skepticism with openness becomes the key to warmer, harmonious relationships post-narcissistic trauma.

REBUILDING TRUST WITHIN AND WITHOUT

Rebuilding trust after surviving a narcissistic relationship is a personal journey anchored in self-trust as the foundation. Strengthening your sense of self-worth and reinforcing boundaries become the bedrock, fostering a feeling of safety and empowerment. Gradually learning to trust others involves

- navigating the intricacies of overcoming the negative inner voice,
- discerning trustworthy traits, and
- embracing effective communication as a tool for rebuilding trust.

Self-Trust – The Foundation

Trust, though innate, is not freely given—it must be earned. Your actions carry more weight than words, and consistency is the key (McDowell, 2022). The crucial aspect often overlooked is self-trust—the silent dialogue with your inner self. It is about feeling secure in your choices and having a deep connection to your purpose, needs, talents, and desires. When entering new relationships, be it with others or yourself, cultivating a sense of safety becomes the first step in the beautiful choreography of trust. Trust in yourself and in your "Why" forms the backbone of making choices that align with your most authentic self and ultimately lead to a life filled with purpose and fulfillment.

Steps to Gradually Trusting Others

Rebuilding trust in others involves navigating three essential factors: overcoming negative inner voices, learning to trust again, and discerning the trustworthiness of others. Let's delve into each factor for a comprehensive understanding.

Overcoming the Negative Inner Voice

Navigating the labyrinth of a negative inner voice requires finesse. Let's discover the key steps to overcome the negative inner voice (Tartakovsky, 2014).

1. **Practice Volume Control Technique:** Recall instances where external sounds diminished. Mentally cover your ears or submerge them metaphorically to silence the negative inner voice.
2. **Positive Inquiry Strategy:** Pose positive questions to counteract negativity. Redirect your focus by asking, "What else can I enjoy right now?" or similar inquiries.
3. **Thought Linking With Self-Acceptance:** Utilize emotional freedom techniques by linking opposing thoughts with self-acceptance. For instance, say, "Even though I have failed repeatedly, I deeply and completely accept myself."
4. **Trust the Gradual Change Process:** Embrace the understanding that your inner voice can be tamed, not silenced. Trust the process of gradual change, allowing yourself to navigate relationships with newfound assurance.

Learning to Trust Again

Distrust often stems from past wounds or learned cultural attitudes. To break this cycle, seek closure for past wounds, defining your own values independent of a skewed past. Act proactively and assertively, confronting fears rather than anticipating them. Seek reassurance when triggered, reaching out for support. Experiment with taking words at face value, gradually rebuilding a solid foundation for relationships. Professional help can serve as a guide in this journey of rewiring your trust patterns.

Knowing if Someone Is Trustworthy

Trustworthy individuals exhibit consistent behavior; they show compassion, humility, and respect for boundaries. They readily compromise, avoid materialism, and are comfortable being themselves. A trustworthy person values time, shows gratitude, and practices transparency. They confide in you, avoid gossip, and are perpetual learners. They facilitate connections and are supportive without ulterior motives. Knowing these signs reveals the keepers in your life, fostering relationships built on trust and authenticity.

Here's the checklist to spot if someone is worth your trust (Thibodeaux, 2020):

1. **Consistency is Key:** A trustworthy individual maintains consistent behavior across various situations. Their words and actions align, creating a reliable pattern you can depend on.

2. **Compassion and Humility Shine Through:** Genuine compassion and humility demonstrate that a person values others and doesn't consider themselves superior. Such traits indicate a selfless nature, reducing the likelihood of betrayal or self-serving actions.

3. **Respect for Boundaries:** Trustworthy people respect personal boundaries. They don't impose their will on others and understand the importance of consent, steering clear of controlling behaviors.

4. **Willingness to Compromise:** Small sacrifices showcase a two-way street of trust. A trustworthy individual is ready to give a little, understanding the reciprocal nature of building a trustworthy relationship.

5. **Relaxed Demeanor:** A person at ease typically has nothing to hide. A trustworthy individual's calm and relaxed demeanor reflects honesty and openness, contributing to a comfortable and authentic relationship.

6. **Punctuality Reflects Respect:** Trustworthy individuals value your time, avoiding last-minute cancellations or tardiness. Their commitment to promises and punctuality demonstrates a sincere regard for your convenience.

7. **Gratitude and Teamwork:** Trustworthy individuals acknowledge the value of teamwork and express gratitude. They share credit where it's due, fostering a collaborative and supportive environment.

8. **Truth and Transparency:** Transparency matters to trustworthy people. They don't withhold information or

manipulate facts. Instead, they prioritize honesty, even when it involves sharing potentially uncomfortable truths.

9. **Confiding Indicates Trust:** Confiding in you, flaws and all, demonstrates trust. When someone opens up, they trust you with their vulnerabilities and encourage openness in return.

10. **Not Driven by Materialism:** Trustworthy individuals prioritize people over possessions. They are not driven solely by material gains and are willing to sacrifice for the benefit of others.

11. **Being Right Comes From Research:** Trustworthy people value truth and do their homework. Their commitment to research ensures they provide accurate information, contributing to a track record of being right.

12. **Avoids Gossip and Rumors:** Trustworthy individuals steer clear of gossip and rumors. They seek information from reliable sources, avoiding negativity that can damage relationships.

13. **Commitment to Continuous Learning:** A trustworthy person acknowledges that learning is a lifelong journey. Their commitment to personal development means they are willing to share newfound knowledge and resources.

14. **Facilitates Connections:** Trustworthy individuals introduce you to their social circle, emphasizing your importance. The more people they connect you with, the more likely they are to be open about who they are.

15. **Consistent Support:** Trustworthy people offer support without hidden agendas, even when they don't need anything in return. Their consistent presence in both good and challenging times establishes them as dependable allies in your life.

Communication as a Trust-Building Tool

Grounded in these principles, effective communication becomes a conduit for rebuilding trust. It's a gradual process in which words and actions weave a narrative of dependability and authenticity. In the aftermath of a narcissistic relationship, rebuilding trust becomes a delicate dance. Effective communication emerges as a powerful tool to mend the fractures left behind.

1. **Clarity in Commitments:** Instead of making grand promises, communicate clearly about what you can commit to. Avoiding overcommitment fosters a sense of reliability and sets the foundation for rebuilding trust.

2. **Consistency Is Key:** Regularly demonstrating your presence and commitment reinforces trust, especially in challenging times. Consistent communication, whether through words or actions, becomes a beacon of dependability.

3. **Active Participation in Teams:** In team dynamics, active involvement and transparent communication build trust. Actively listening, respectfully providing feedback, and embracing a collaborative approach signal a commitment to trustworthiness.

4. **Honesty as the Cornerstone:** Upholding truth strengthens trust, even in uncomfortable situations. Honest communication, devoid of deceit, forms a bridge toward rebuilding trust post-narcissistic experiences.

5. **Openness About Emotions:** Sharing your emotions openly conveys authenticity. Emotional intelligence plays a pivotal role; acknowledging feelings and expressing care fosters a connection, gradually reconstructing trust.

6. **Avoiding Self-Promotion:** Recognition and appreciation of others' efforts contribute to trust-building. Steer away from constant self-promotion, as a genuine acknowledgment of team members enhances trust within relationships.

7. **Staying True to Values:** Trust is fortified when actions align with personal values. The courage to do what you believe is right, even if it contradicts popular opinions, builds a foundation of trust.

8. **Admission of Mistakes:** Transparency in admitting mistakes showcases vulnerability. Instead of concealing errors, open acknowledgment fosters relatability, demonstrating that everyone is prone to missteps.

NURTURING HEALTHY RELATIONSHIPS

Nurturing healthy relationships is an ongoing, intentional effort. It is a dance where partners move in harmony, adjusting steps when needed and finding beauty in the shared rhythm of life.

Recognizing and Fostering Healthy Dynamics

A healthy relationship is not a utopian fantasy; it's a dynamic, evolving connection where both individuals contribute to a shared journey of growth, understanding, and joy. Here is a glimpse into the vibrant canvas of a healthy relationship:

1. **Communication That Dances:** Picture this—a couple sitting on the couch, not just exchanging words but engaging in a dance of communication. They share their thoughts openly, listen actively, and understand each other's unspoken emotions. It is a dialogue that builds bridges, not walls.

2. **Respecting Individual Beats:** Imagine a scenario where personal space is not a distant concept but a cherished reality. Each partner respects the other's solo beats—pursuing hobbies, spending time with friends, or enjoying moments of solitude. In this dance, individuality is not lost but celebrated.

3. **Conflict Resolution, a Graceful Waltz:** Envision a disagreement turning into a graceful waltz of compromise and understanding. Healthy relationships navigate conflicts with respect, finding solutions that honor both perspectives. It's not about winning but about evolving together.

4. **Shared Dreams, a Symphony of Unity:** Think of a couple whose dreams entwine, creating a symphony of shared aspirations. They support each other's goals, celebrating victories together and providing solace in

defeats. In this harmony, the relationship becomes a shared canvas of dreams.

5. **Laughter, the Joyful Choreography:** Consider a moment where laughter echoes through the rooms. A healthy relationship finds joy in shared jokes, light banter, and the simple act of finding humor in life's quirks. Laughter becomes the choreography of happiness.

Allowing People Closer – Love and Connection, Post-Abuse

Embarking on the path of love after surviving an abusive relationship is a courageous journey, a testament to resilience and healing. Here is a glimpse into the nuanced dance of love and connection post-abuse (Davis, 2021):

1. **The Healing Odyssey:** Imagine navigating the labyrinth of post-abuse healing, with resources initially abundant but waning as time progresses. The journey involves rediscovering oneself, reclaiming power, and acknowledging that healing is an ongoing process, not a one-time event.

2. **Misunderstood Scars:** Consider the challenge of explaining emotional and mental abuse to those who haven't walked that path. It's a struggle to articulate the scars that run deep beneath the surface, where words often fall short, and expressing emotions becomes daunting.

3. **Yearning for a Healing Savior:** Blame Disney for the notion that a partner should be a healing savior. Post-abuse, that subconscious desire emerges, wanting the new partner to mend all wounds. Yet, the reality is that true healing comes from within, and expecting a partner to be a cure-all sets an unfair expectation.

4. **Guilt's Stealthy Intrusion:** Picture guilt, a lingering ghost from past abuse, infiltrating a new relationship. Seeking constant approval, doubting every action, and navigating the minefield of guilt manipulation, guilt becomes an unwanted companion, casting shadows on self-worth.

5. **The Symphony of Communication:** Envision the importance of communication in a healing relationship but acknowledge the need for personal growth first. Communicating from a place of anxiety or fear without blaming the partner becomes a delicate art. Sharing past experiences and current struggles requires a calm, centered approach.

6. **The Journey to Healing's Summit:** Picture a landscape where healing is not just possible but transformative. Acknowledging the desire for change becomes the catalyst for a journey filled with personalized tools, support networks, and the creation of one's narrative—a journey that turns pain into power.

7. **Challenging the Notion of Difficult Healing:** Challenge the misconception that healing must be an arduous, uphill battle. Imagine turning the healing process into a game, surrounded by a team of supportive

allies who redefine the narrative. Reject the notion that healing has to be painful; instead, it can be a joyful, freeing experience.

As we conclude this chapter, we've realized that trust is the foundation upon which we rebuild our connections to the world and rebuild ourselves after a complex relationship.

CHAPTER 8
PLANNING FOR A FUTURE POST-ABUSE

The best way to predict the future is to create it.

PETER DRUCKER

In a quiet moment of reflection, Clara closed her eyes and let her mind paint a vivid picture of a future unburdened by the chains of her past. In this dream sequence, she saw herself standing tall and confident, basking in the warm glow of self-love and acceptance. The air was filled with a sense of freedom and security, like a gentle embrace that whispered, "You are safe now." Surrounded by supportive friends and pursuing her passion, Clara felt the exhilarating sensation of being in control of her destiny. It was a vision that embodied the essence of feeling safe and loved—a beacon of hope guiding her toward the promising future she was determined to create.

ENVISIONING A BRIGHT FUTURE: PAINTING THE CANVAS OF YOUR TOMORROW

Embarking on the journey of envisioning a future post-abuse is akin to picking up a brush and painting the canvas of your tomorrow. Let's explore the vibrant hues that define this transformative process.

Stages of Recovery: Navigating Toward a Future of Freedom

Embarking on the journey of recovery after narcissistic abuse, you find solace in understanding the three transformative stages outlined by French psychologist Pierre Janet and further refined by Judith Herman. These stages, though challenging, propel you toward a future where the shackles of the past loosen, allowing you to integrate the lessons learned and build a life that radiates with the freedom you deserve (Kippert, 2023).

Stage 1: Safety and Stabilization

In this initial phase, you, dear reader, grapple with feelings of unease, both within your own skin and in your relationships. The everyday emotions that once seemed elusive become a battle-ground. Yet, this struggle is not in vain—it's the groundwork for rebuilding a sanctuary of safety. It's a process spanning months or even years, where you gradually rediscover what it means to feel secure.

Stage 2: Remembrance and Mourning

As you traverse the second phase, the shadows of trauma begin to take shape, and words and emotions intertwine to make sense of the pain. This stage, best navigated with the guidance of a compassionate counselor or therapist, invites you to mourn the losses tethered to the trauma. It's a sacred space for grieving, allowing emotions to flow freely, cleansing the wounds of the past

Stage 3: Reconnection and Integration

In the final stage, envision yourself not as a victim but as a resilient survivor. Acknowledge the impact of victimization, yet embrace the profound truth that trauma no longer defines you. Here, you redefine yourself amid meaningful relationships, forging a new identity. Some may discover a healing mission—mentoring or advocating for others—becoming a beacon of inspiration for those on a similar journey.

Embracing Hope in Dark Times: A Guiding Light

In the aftermath of a narcissistic relationship, hope emerges as a transformative force, offering a glimpse of a brighter future. It's not wishful thinking but a belief in the possibility of positive change. Hope acts as a catalyst, inspires actionable steps, and helps manage stress and navigate challenges. Resilient and grounded in reality, hope becomes a powerful companion, guiding you through adversity and fueling the pursuit of a fulfilling future.

Setting Goals and Aspirations

In the aftermath of a narcissistic relationship, setting personal and career goals becomes a pivotal step in reclaiming control and envisioning a brighter future. Before embarking on this journey, ask yourself why each goal truly matters to you. The essence of your aspirations should resonate deeply, aligning with your authentic desires rather than external expectations (Dixon, 2022).

After identifying your "why," assess the market and demand for your ambitions, conducting thorough research to ensure their viability. Consider the time, training, and patience required to align your aspirations with your personality, skills, and the practicalities of your life. Remember, your dreams don't adhere to deadlines—navigate them at your pace, ensuring a fulfilling and sustainable post-abuse narrative.

Embracing the Possibility of Happiness: A Personal Odyssey

In the aftermath of a narcissistic relationship, discovering the potency of intense positive emotions like joy becomes a transformative endeavor. These emotions not only fortify the immune system and shield the heart from trauma but also serve as a beacon of resilience and success. Amid the trials and tribulations, joy emerges as a steadfast companion, reminding you that defeat is not etched in the sanctuary of your mind. Even in the darkest moments, joy can be claimed and welcomed, serving as a triumphant flame against gathering darkness. To invoke joy, value everyday opportunities that naturally unfold, whether it's marveling at the sun or reveling in the pleasure of a simple sneeze. As you accumulate experiences of joy, the process becomes more accessible, offering a refuge and a source of light in the stormiest of skies.

PRACTICAL STEPS TO A NEW BEGINNING

Independence and Life Planning

Embarking on a new beginning post-narcissistic abuse is a journey of self-discovery and empowerment. To reclaim independence and foster fulfillment, several practical steps pave the way, including financial planning, exploring career opportunities, and surrounding yourself with positive influences.

Financial independence is not just about accumulating wealth; it's a powerful tool that can unlock the doors to a life aligned with your deepest goals and aspirations. Here's your guide to navigating the intertwined paths of financial freedom and life planning by following FIRE (Financial Independence, Retire Early) principles (Flamingo, 2022).

Discovering Your True Goals

Before delving into a FIRE (Financial Independence, Retire Early) strategy, take a moment for introspection. What truly brings you joy and fulfillment? Understanding your life goals lays the foundation for a plan that goes beyond monetary pursuits.

The Pitfall of Financial-Only Plans

Financial plans alone will not lead to lasting happiness. While FIRE provides the freedom to control your time, it's the alignment with your goals that brings genuine satisfaction. Recognize that money is a means to an end, not the end itself.

Learning from Experience

A failed attempt at FIRE highlighted the importance of not just running away from the unpleasant but seeking true fulfillment. Time, money, and freedom may not guarantee happiness without a clear understanding of who you are and what you genuinely desire.

Holistic Life Planning

Separating financial plans from life plans can lead to dissatisfaction. Incorporate life planning into your financial journey. Identify your goals, values, and passions, ensuring that financial strategies align with your overarching life plan.

Avoiding Procrastination and Excuses

Delaying happiness until financial goals are achieved is a common pitfall. Don't let FIRE become a distraction; instead, set up a financial system that empowers you to pursue your dreams confidently.

Unlocking Educational and Career Opportunities

Embarking on a journey of educational and career opportunities is a transformative endeavor. Remember, the journey is as significant as the destination—embrace it, learn from it, and let it shape a future filled with educational and career fulfillment. Here is a personalized framework to guide you through the process, ensuring engagement, growth, and success:

Acknowledge and Process Your Story

Just as in post-traumatic growth, the first step is acknowledging your narrative. Reflect on your educational and career journey—acknowledge the challenges, setbacks, and victories. Processing your story is the foundation for embracing the potential ahead.

Reflect on Your Beliefs and Values

Educational and career pursuits often intersect with our core beliefs. Take a moment to reflect on how your past experiences have shaped your beliefs and values. Use this insight to redefine your priorities and align your educational and career goals with your authentic self.

Seek Guidance and Professional Support

Recognize that seeking help is a strength, not a weakness. Just as trained professionals assist in processing trauma, career counselors and educational advisors provide invaluable support. Seek guidance from those experienced in navigating educational landscapes and career paths.

Recognize Your Unique Strengths

Amid challenges, acknowledge your strengths, resilience, and courage. These attributes have carried you through experiences, showcasing your adaptability. Recognizing these strengths empowers you and serves as a foundation for future growth and success.

Craft a Personalized Timeline

Understand that growth takes time. Establish a personalized timeline for your educational and career pursuits. It's okay to evolve gradually, allowing yourself to absorb lessons, acquire skills, and adapt to new realities. Patience is key to realizing the positive aspects of your journey.

Surrounding Yourself With Positive Influences

Creating a positive environment around you is more than just a mood booster—it's a transformative force for your brain and overall well-being. Here's a practical guide focused on surrounding yourself with positive influences (Whalen-Harris, 2023):

Harness the Power of Positive Thinking

Understand the science behind positive thinking. Embrace joy and gratitude, triggering the release of dopamine and serotonin in your brain. This feels good and creates a positive feedback loop, reinforcing optimistic patterns.

Boost Mental Health

Cultivate positivity to reduce stress, anxiety, and depression. A positive attitude becomes a powerful tool in facing challenges, enhancing your mental resilience and overall well-being.

Strengthen Relationships

Positivity is contagious. Foster stronger connections with friends, family, and colleagues by radiating positivity. Build a supportive environment that encourages personal and collective growth.

Enhance Resilience

Face setbacks with a positive outlook. Resilience flourishes when you maintain optimism, bouncing back from challenges stronger than before. Embrace the belief that setbacks are stepping stones to success.

Invest in Physical Health

The benefits of positivity extend to your physical health. Improve your immune system, reduce inflammation, and lower the risk of chronic diseases by maintaining a positive mindset.

Promote Happiness and Well-being

A positive mindset isn't just about facing challenges—it's about finding joy in everyday experiences. Appreciate the good things in life, savor moments of happiness, and let positivity become a constant companion.

Everyday Practices for Positivity

Now, let's delve into practical tips that fit seamlessly into your daily life:

1. **Stay Connected:** Cultivate social connections. Reach out to loved ones regularly, fostering a supportive network that acts as a buffer against life's challenges.

2. **Gratitude Journal:** Start a gratitude journal. Write down three things daily that you are grateful for. This practice supports a resilient "psychological immune system."

3. **Mindful Meditation:** Embrace mindfulness. Meditate, focus on your breath, and reflect on the positive aspects of your surroundings. Ground yourself to respond effectively to circumstances.

4. **Nourish Your Body:** Eat well-balanced, nutrient-rich meals. A healthy diet contributes to a balanced mood, combating feelings of depression and anxiety.

5. **Prioritize Quality Sleep:** Ensure sufficient and quality sleep. Poor sleep worsens mental health symptoms, making adequate rest a crucial element of your positivity journey.

6. **Limit Screen Time:** Reduce excessive screen time. A conscious effort to disconnect contributes to higher psychological well-being.

7. **Stay Active:** Incorporate enjoyable physical activities into your routine. Exercise, especially outdoors, significantly reduces depression and anxiety.

8. **Practice Kindness:** Be kind in small ways. Offer compliments, show empathy, and listen actively. Acts of kindness release oxytocin, fostering happiness and well-being.

9. **Navigating Challenges With Positivity:** In difficult times, proactively limit stress triggers. Develop coping strategies and surround yourself with a network of trusted individuals who support your goals. Cultivate

positivity as a daily practice, and let it guide you through both triumphs and challenges.

GUARDING AGAINST RELAPSE

In the complex dance of recovery, acknowledging the possibility of relapse, understanding its dynamics, and having a robust prevention and recovery plan in place can fortify the journey toward lasting well-being. Every day spent in recovery is significant, forming an indelible part of the path toward a healthier, more resilient self.

Recognizing Potential Triggers

Trauma responses are as unique as fingerprints, making the identification of triggers a deeply individualized journey. Unraveling the complicated web of triggers involves understanding that they can manifest in various forms, often surprising us with their subtlety. For instance, certain sounds, like sirens, music, or gunshots, can induce unwanted responses, creating a sense of unease even in seemingly secure environments. Triggers can also manifest through sights, smells, situations, or emotions, each linked to past traumas, unveiling layers of emotional responses and memories (Wright, 2021).

Identifying Triggers

Triggers might seem unpredictable, but once identified, connections between events, feelings, or sights become apparent. A journal can be a powerful tool. Record thoughts, feelings, and environmental factors during flashbacks or panic episodes.

What did you hear? See? Smell? How were you feeling? Identifying patterns in the journal can unveil recurring triggers.

Next Steps

When traumatic events cast a long shadow over your life, adversely affecting your psychological and physical health, seeking trauma-focused treatment is a proactive step.

Evidence-based treatments like prolonged exposure (PE) therapy and cognitive processing therapy (CPT) can significantly reduce the frequency of trigger effects, such as intrusive memories.

Maintaining Boundaries With Potential Narcissists

Maintaining boundaries with potential narcissists is crucial for preserving your well-being and sanity. As discussed in Chapter 5, it's essential to establish clear limits, communicate assertively, and prioritize self-care to navigate relationships with narcissistic individuals while safeguarding your mental and emotional health.

Staying Connected When You Do Not Have A Support System

When trapped in an abusive situation without a support system, the isolation can feel overwhelming. The abuser's tactics, such as cutting off connections, can intensify this loneliness. Consider looking beyond your immediate circle to potential allies like caring co-workers or acquaintances to combat this. Volunteer yourself for care homes and public therapy to connect with individuals who share a passion for helping. Ultimately, recognize your own strength as a vital component of your support network to empower yourself to break free from isolation.

Our past may shape us, but our future is ours to define, and progress will not be a lonely one. In the next section, we examine the power of community support.

CHAPTER 9
THE ROLE OF COMMUNITY IN RECOVERY

We are all healers of each other. Look at David Spiegel's fascinating study of putting people together in a support group and seeking that some people in it live twice as long as other people who are not in a support group. I asked David what went on in those groups, and he said that people just cared about each other. Nothing big, no deep psychological stuff—people just cared about each other. The reality is that healing happens between people.

NAOMI REMEN

The support group gathered in a cozy community center, each member carrying the weight of their unique traumas. As the meeting unfolded, a courageous soul, Emma, bravely shared her harrowing journey of surviving narcissistic abuse. Her words echoed through the room, painting a vivid picture of pain and resilience. Surprisingly, nods of understanding and empathetic glances circulated as others recognized fragments of their own stories in Emma's narrative. In that sacred space, collective strength emerged, transforming isolated struggles into a united front against the aftermath of abuse. It was a poignant reminder that, indeed, healing happens between people, echoing the profound wisdom of Rachel Naomi Remen.

THE IMPORTANCE OF A SUPPORT NETWORK

Imagine navigating the labyrinth of trauma alone—a daunting journey that becomes significantly more bearable with the presence of a support network. This safety net isn't just about shared burdens; it's a lifeline that reaffirms you're not alone. Picture survivors of narcissistic abuse coming together, understanding the weight of silence lifted as they connect over shared narratives in a therapeutic embrace. It's a reminder that the path to recovery is not solitary but a collective triumph over adversity.

Not Journeying Alone – Surviving Trauma After Abuse

In the aftermath of trauma, the path to healing can seem like an isolated expedition. Nevertheless, the heartening truth emerges—survivors of abuse find strength in shared experiences. Meet Christina, a resilient soul who once felt adrift in the aftermath of narcissistic abuse. In the supportive embrace of a survivor community, Christina discovered kindred spirits, individuals who echoed her pain and triumphs. This camaraderie transformed her isolation into a shared odyssey, proving that the journey from victim to survivor is not solitary.

Furthermore, the notion of not journeying alone extends beyond human connections. Many survivors find solace in their spiritual beliefs. It's an intimate connection with a higher power, an unspoken understanding that in the darkest moments, there is divine companionship. Much like Christina, who found reassurance in her faith, survivors realize they are not merely supported by each other but also by something greater—a force that weaves through their recovery, reminding them that, even in the loneliest moments, they are never truly alone (Lopez, 2018).

The Therapeutic Role of Shared Narratives

In the journey of coping with trauma, shared narratives become a powerful balm for wounded souls. Take Steve, for instance, who bore the weight of his mother's narcissism. As he stepped into a group therapy session, he found solace in the collective tales of survivors who, like him, navigated the tumultuous waters of psychological abuse. The psychologist leading the session provided a roadmap, offering scientifically proven strategies for managing each member's specific challenges (Johnson, 2019).

The magic unfolded in the diverse fabric of the group—individuals from varied backgrounds sharing their triumphs and strategies. Steve, once isolated in the echoes of his own pain, discovered a chorus of voices harmonizing with his struggle. The group acted as a support network and as a classroom where members exchanged strategies, providing a kaleidoscope of approaches to confront their shared adversities.

This therapeutic alliance transcended mere support—it became a cornerstone of growth. The shared narratives, carefully guided by professionals, became a collective journey toward healing, a testament to the transformative power embedded in the stories we courageously shared.

Community Resources for Survivors

The following resources, among others, play a crucial role in creating a safety net for survivors, offering avenues for support, empowerment, and healing (NCADV, 2023).

The National Domestic Violence Hotline
 Hotline: 1-800-799-7233 (SAFE) | Website: https://www. ndvh.org,

A lifeline for immediate assistance, providing support and resources to those facing domestic violence.

National Dating Abuse Helpline
Hotline: 1-866-331-9474 | Website: https://www.loveisrespec t.org.

Offering assistance to those experiencing dating abuse and fostering healthy relationships through education and support.

National Child Abuse Hotline/Childhelp

Hotline: 1-800-4-A-CHILD (1-800-422-4453) | Website: https://www.childhelp.org

A crucial resource providing intervention, support, and information for child abuse victims and concerned individuals.

National Sexual Assault Hotline

Hotline: 1-800-656-4673 (HOPE) | Website: https://www.rainn.org.

Empowering survivors of sexual assault and offering a safe space for healing and guidance.

National Suicide Prevention Lifeline

Hotline: 1-800-273-8255 (TALK) | Website: https://www.suicidepreventionlifeline.org

A critical support network for individuals in crisis, providing confidential assistance and prevention resources.

National Center for Victims of Crime

Contact: 1-202-467-8700 | Website: https://www.victimsofcrime.org.

Dedicated to supporting victims of various crimes, advocating for their rights, and offering resources.

National Human Trafficking Resource Center/Polaris Project
Call: 1-888-373-7888 | Text: HELP to 233733 | Website: https://
www.polarisproject.org

Combating human trafficking by providing assistance, resources, and a helpline for victims.

National Network for Immigrant and Refugee Rights
Contact: 1-510-465-1984 | Website: https://www.nnirr.org.

Advocating for immigrant and refugee rights and offering support and resources to those in need.

National Coalition for the Homeless
Contact: 1-202-737-6444 | Website: https://www.nationalhome less.org.

Aiding individuals facing homelessness, providing resources, and advocating for their rights.

National Resource Center on Domestic Violence
Contact: 1-800-537-2238 | Websites: https://www.nrcdv.org and https://www.vawnet.org.

A comprehensive resource center offering information, support, and tools for domestic violence survivors.

ENGAGING WITH SUPPORTIVE COMMUNITIES

Support groups become sanctuaries where individuals healing from narcissistic abuse find solace. From online forums to local gatherings, these communities provide refuge. Consider the courage it takes to join, where anonymity often gives way to profound connections. Resources abound—lists of potential support groups and how to connect—emphasizing the diverse avenues available. Within these circles, the value of family and friends in recovery becomes evident, weaving a broader safety net that extends beyond formal groups.

The Benefits of Support Groups

Support groups, whether peer-led or professionally facilitated, provide a vital space for individuals to share their stories, experiences, and lives, fostering connections that alleviate the burden of isolation and loneliness. While open to anyone, these groups often revolve around specific topics like depression, family, divorce, grief, and more. The key is to find a supportive community that aligns with your current situation (Olivine, 2023).

Choosing and Accessing Support

Choosing the right support group is crucial, and it's normal if the first one doesn't feel quite right. Feeling comfortable is essential, so exploring different groups can help identify the best fit. Online support groups, discussion boards, and blogs have become invaluable additions, particularly when in-person options are limited.

Mental Health America's support community through Inspire is a noteworthy online resource, offering a platform to connect on various mental health topics.

Local Support Groups

You can find local support groups by contacting your local Mental Health America affiliate. The National Mental Health Consumers' Self-Help Group Clearinghouse also maintains a Directory of Consumer-Driven Services, listing peer-run organizations across the United States.

Specialized Support Group Resources

Beyond general support, numerous specialized resources cater to specific challenges. From addiction and anxiety to grief and caregiving, these groups offer targeted assistance. Examples include Alcoholics Anonymous, Alzheimer's Association, Anxiety and Depression Association of America, and many more.

Most Common Support Groups

Several common support groups address a wide array of challenges, including addiction, anxiety, depression, caregiving, grief, and more. These groups provide a structured environment where members share experiences, learn coping skills, and receive expert insights. The following non-exhaustive list contains the most common support groups for victims and survivors (MHA, 2023):

1. **Adult Children of Alcoholics**—Provides support for individuals who grew up in alcoholic or dysfunctional homes.

2. **Al-Anon/Alateen**—Offers support for families and friends of alcoholics through shared experiences and coping strategies.

3. **Anxiety and Depression Association of America (ADAA)**—Peer-led support group under ADAA focusing on individuals dealing with anxiety and depression.

4. **Attention Deficit Disorder Association (ADDA)**—Provides support and resources for individuals with attention deficit disorders.

5. **The Balanced Mind Foundation**—Aids families dealing with mood disorders in children and adolescents through education and support.

6. **Children and Adults with Attention Deficit/Hyperactivity Disorder (CHADD)**—Focuses on ADHD support and education, including parent resources and training.

7. **Co-Dependents Anonymous**—A fellowship supporting individuals in developing healthy, fulfilling relationships.

8. **The Compassionate Friends Grief Support**—Provides support for families grieving the death of a child.

9. **CoSLAA Support Groups for Family and Friends of People with Sex Addiction**—Offers support for those affected by a loved one's sex addiction.

10. **Crisis Text Line**—A free crisis intervention service providing support via text messaging.

11. **Depression and Bipolar Support Alliance (DBSA)**—Provides support, education, and advocacy for individuals with mood disorders.

12. **Dual Diagnosis Rehab Centers**—Offers support to individuals dealing with both mental health and substance abuse conditions.

The Value of Family and Friends in Recovery

While professional-led support groups play a crucial role, the support of family and friends is equally invaluable. Their understanding and encouragement create a holistic support network. In the recovery journey from narcissistic abuse, having loved ones who empathize and stand by you enhances the healing process.

GIVING BACK AND ADVOCACY

Finding life's true purpose is the heartbeat of recovery. The narrative shifts from victim to survivor when one realizes that helping others becomes a powerful tool for personal healing. Advocacy takes root—individuals, once silent, find their voices, raising awareness and understanding about narcissistic abuse. Supporting fellow survivors becomes a reciprocal journey, solidifying the idea that, in recovery, giving back is an integral part of the art and science of healing.

Transforming Pain Into Purpose

Life's journey is laden with challenges, from heartbreaks to health crises, and it's during these tumultuous times that we often question life's purpose. However, amid the struggles lies an opportunity to transform pain into purpose, emerging from the darkness stronger and more resilient than ever before. Exploring the steps that can turn adversity into a source of strength is a transformative journey. Let's explore it together.

Step 1: Allow Yourself to Feel

Embracing the full spectrum of emotions that accompany hardship is the initial step toward healing. Suppressing or avoiding these emotions only delays the recovery process. By acknowledging and allowing yourself to feel sadness, anger, or confusion, you pave the way for genuine healing. For instance, after the loss of a loved one, allowing yourself to grieve openly rather than bottling up emotions can be a cathartic and crucial step in the healing process.

Step 2: Find Perspective

Putting challenges into perspective is a powerful tool for shifting your mindset. Gratitude becomes a guiding light, steering your thoughts from scarcity to abundance. Even in the darkest moments, there are aspects of life to be thankful for, be it the support of loved ones, having a shelter, or simply the gift of life itself.

Step 3: Identify Your Values and Beliefs

Hardships often lead us to question our values and beliefs. Identifying these core aspects of ourselves allows for a deeper understanding of what motivates us. Aligning these values with our current situation helps us make intentional decisions in response to adversity.

Step 4: Reflect and Take Action

Armed with a clear understanding of your values, it's time to reflect on actionable steps. Channeling your struggles through a lens that aligns with your true self and reflects your values allows for intentional and purpose-driven actions.

For example, a person who has experienced poverty may choose to actively contribute to the community by volunteering at a soup kitchen or organizing events that empower those affected by poverty.

Step 5: Find Support

No transformative journey is complete without a support system. Seeking help, whether through therapy or leaning on friends and family, provides outlets for shared burdens and reinforces positive habits.

Advocating for Awareness and Understanding

Victim advocates are unsung heroes, standing alongside those who have faced adversity and providing a voice and a pathway to healing. Their multifaceted roles contribute significantly to fostering awareness and understanding of the challenges victims face. Victim advocates play a vital role in creating a supportive and compassionate society by championing the rights and well-being of those affected. Let's discuss the key benefits of victim advocacy (Hurtado, 2023).

1. **Emotional Support and Trauma Mitigation:** Victim advocates serve as trusted confidants, offering emotional support crucial for victims dealing with trauma's short- and long-term effects on their physical and mental health.

2. **Enhanced Recovery:** Studies have shown that victims who work with advocates experience less violence and depression, highlighting the positive impact of these professionals on the recovery process.

3. **Legal Guidance:** Navigating the complex legal landscape can be challenging for victims. Advocates play a crucial role in helping victims understand their

legal rights and facilitating their participation in the criminal justice process.

4. **Proactive Outreach:** Proactive advocacy engagement increases victims' participation in the legal process, providing greater benefits and resources for their recovery.

Supporting Fellow Survivors on Their Journeys

Embarking on the path of healing after surviving sexual assault or domestic violence requires immense courage. As a friend, family member, or ally, you can significantly impact a survivor's journey. Understanding the right words, actions, and resources is crucial to providing meaningful support. Let's explore the six steps to supporting a survivor, offering comfort and compassion throughout their healing process (Hargitay, 2023).

Listen

Sometimes, the most potent support comes from a listening ear. Allowing survivors to share their stories lessens the burden of isolation, secrecy, and self-blame. Listening, in itself, becomes an act of profound love and understanding.

Validate

Acknowledge the survivor's pain and validate their feelings with compassionate phrases such as "I believe you," "This is not your fault," or "You are not alone." By dispelling victim-blaming myths, you reinforce the survivor's worth and resilience.

1. Nothing you did or could have done differently makes this your fault.
2. The responsibility is on the person who hurt you.
3. No one ever has the right to hurt you.

Ask How You Can Help

Recognizing the survivor's need for regained personal power, ask how you can support them. Avoid pushing them into actions they may not be ready for, respecting their journey toward recovery.

Know Where to Point for Help

Offer options and guide survivors to additional help. Share national resources that can connect them to local support services, ensuring they have the information to make informed decisions.

Keep an Open Heart

Acknowledge the potential length of the healing journey, and assure survivors that you are available for ongoing conversations. Maintaining an open heart creates a safe space for survivors to share their experiences whenever they feel ready.

Care for Yourself

Supporting survivors can take an emotional toll. Acknowledge your own limits and practice self-care. Taking time for yourself ensures you can continue offering compassionate support without becoming overwhelmed.

Taking care of yourself is paramount. If you find yourself too tired to listen with care and compassion, or if you are sated with your own emotions in response to another's trauma, you cannot be your best self in your supportive role.

After delving into the power of community and support groups, it's important to fortify our minds for sustainable change. Building and strengthening a more positive mindset takes time and should be part of your everyday lifestyle. The following chapter shows you how.

CHAPTER 10
EMBRACING THE NEW SELF

In order to love who you are, you cannot hate the experiences that shaped you.

ANDRÉA DYKSTRA

Letter to My Younger Self

Dear Younger Self,

As I pen down these words, I am overwhelmed with emotions, reflecting on our journey. The path has been arduous, filled with shadows of pain and echoes of a past we once thought would define us forever. Nevertheless, here we are, on the other side of healing, stronger and more resilient than ever.

In those dark moments, it might have seemed impossible to imagine a future beyond the anguish that enveloped us. The scars we bear, both visible and hidden, tell stories of survival, courage, and the unwavering will to reclaim our lives. Those scars, my dear, are not marks of weakness but badges of strength, a testament to the battles we faced and conquered.

Through the labyrinth of recovery, we reached milestones that once felt insurmountable. Each step forward was a victory, a proclamation that we refused to let the shadows of the past dictate our future. The advice we received along the way, the support that cradled us, and the resilience we discovered within ourselves became the guiding stars leading us out of the darkness.

As I look ahead, I see a horizon teeming with new possibilities. Once shrouded in uncertainty, the future now beckons with the promise of joy, growth, and fulfillment. Our mindset has shifted. We've learned that the profound art of self-love in cultivating joy every day propels us forward, urging us to embrace life's potential and seize every opportunity that comes our way.

In cultivating joy every day, we've learned the profound art of self-love. It is a continuous journey, a practice that nurtures our spirit and reinforces the belief that we deserve happiness and peace. The empowerment affirmations we now hold dear are not just words; they are the mantras that echo our newfound strength.

As I stand on this precipice of transformation, I want you to know, dear younger self, that the metamorphosis was not easy, but it was undoubtedly worth it. The pain has sculpted us into a masterpiece of resilience, and the scars have become a canvas painted with the vibrant colors of survival.

So, let us celebrate this new self, forged in the crucible of adversity. Let us honor the journey, for it has led us to a place of self-discovery, empowerment, and unyielding hope. The echoes of our past no longer define us; instead, they serve as a poignant reminder of the strength that resides within us.

With love and resilience,

Your Future Self

REFLECTING ON THE JOURNEY

In the sensitive process of emotional abuse recovery, reflection becomes a pivotal compass, guiding survivors toward the new selves they're destined to become. Imagine this journey as a de-programming from the toxic narratives that once infiltrated every facet of your being. Victims, akin to members of a cult, find themselves gradually stripped of self-esteem, confidence, and even sanity.

Reflecting on the Milestones Achieved

Embarking on the journey of rediscovering self-worth, let's illuminate the milestones that shape our path, casting aside shadows and welcoming the emergence of a resilient survivor. In this profound voyage, we first unravel the insidious illusion of guilt and self-blame, recognizing them not as personal failures but as weapons wielded by abusers. The journey takes a triumphant turn as we navigate the challenging terrain of establishing boundaries and standing tall against past manipulation (Cheyette, 2021).

Reflecting on self-compassion, we witness the blossoming of kindness within, once overshadowed by internal criticism. Breaking the silence and seeking support becomes a courageous shift from isolation to shared strength. Each step forward is a celebration of incremental growth, a testament to our unwavering resilience in triumphing over adversity. Join me in acknowledging these milestones as beacons lighting our way to a future brimming with possibilities.

Honoring the Scars and the Stories They Tell: A Post-Recovery Celebration

As survivors stand on post-recovery shores, they find themselves adorned with scars, each telling a story of resilience, growth, and triumph. Honoring these scars takes on a new significance, transcending mere acknowledgment and embracing them as badges of strength. While the assumption is that this stage marks a milestone, the journey continues, and further reinforcement is paramount (Herman, 2021).

Symbolism of Scars

In the tapestry of healing, scars are not blemishes to be concealed; they are symbols etched with profound meaning. Each scar narrates a chapter—a testament to the battles and victories we have won. Survivors are encouraged to view these marks not as wounds but as emblems of their journey toward reclaiming autonomy.

The Uniqueness of Journeys

It's imperative to recognize that everyone's journey is a unique odyssey shaped by personal experiences and intricacies. While some may find themselves on the precipice of complete healing, others may seek additional support and reinforcement. Acknowledging that diverse paths exist reinforces the importance of tailoring strategies to individual needs.

Further Strengthening and Development

Post-recovery is not a static destination but a dynamic state of continual growth. Honoring scars involves a commitment to further strengthening and development. Survivors are encouraged to explore new avenues of self-discovery, delve into uncharted territories of personal empowerment, and fortify the foundations of their newfound resilience.

Community and Continued Support

In this phase, the significance of community and continued support becomes paramount. Whether through support groups, therapy, or trusted relationships, survivors are urged to seek and embrace ongoing reinforcement. Individual journeys are better shared. The collective wisdom and experiences within a supportive community serve as pillars that bolster individual journeys.

Shifting Perspectives

Honoring scars necessitates a shift in perspective—from seeing them as remnants of pain to perceiving them as badges of courage. The scars become a canvas on which survivors paint stories of endurance, metamorphosis, and triumph. Embracing this shift cultivates a mindset of empowerment, fostering a narrative of strength derived from adversity.

Recognizing Personal Growth and Transformation

Embarking on your adventure of personal growth and transformation is like setting sail in uncharted waters guided by the compass of your unique essence. Acknowledging your personal growth involves a holistic exploration, delving into the realms of your physical, emotional, social, and financial well-being. Your past, though weathered, does not dictate; it is a canvas of events that forged your resilience.

Cultivating consistent healthy habits, fostering your supportive team, and embracing discomfort as a catalyst define this transformative journey. In this labyrinth of growth, celebrate your progress, maintain your steady pace, and recognize your true allies light the way, emphasizing that your personal growth is an ongoing journey, not just a destination. So, set sail confidently, and let your unique essence be your guiding star.

THE FUTURE IS BRIGHT

As you stand at the threshold of your future, it's essential to recognize the brightness that awaits you after navigating the shadows of narcissistic abuse. Setting your sights on new horizons, you're not merely a survivor but a resilient individual with boundless potential. Embracing life's opportunities becomes a beacon guiding you forward as the growth mindset instilled through your healing journey propels you into a future brimming with possibilities. Cultivating joy in the everyday becomes a conscious choice, a testament to the empowerment you've gained in transcending past challenges. Remember, the journey doesn't end here; it unfolds into a narrative of triumph, resilience, and the radiant light of your redefined self.

Setting Sights on New Horizons

As you embark on the journey of setting your sights on new horizons, envision a path illuminated by the radiance of a positive mindset. Much like the ABC (Adversity-Belief-Consequences) model, where your beliefs shape the consequences of your experiences, consider adversity not as a roadblock but as a stepping stone to growth. The challenges you've faced become the raw materials for a stronger foundation, and your beliefs in resilience and self-worth become the guiding stars.

As you navigate uncharted territories, let the power of a positive mindset be your compass. Let it steer and empower you to shape the narrative of your own triumph. The horizon ahead is painted with the hues of possibilities. With each step, you rewrite your story with newfound strength and belief in a future that reflects your unwavering resilience.

Embracing Life's Potential and Opportunities

In the aftermath of abuse, the journey toward embracing life's potential and opportunities becomes a powerful odyssey of self-discovery. It involves not only healing from the wounds inflicted but also learning how to respond better to life's challenges. Imagine reframing your mindset, shifting from reactive responses to a solution-focused approach, unlocking doors to a happier existence. It's like sculpting a masterpiece from the shards of adversity.

In this transformative process, finding a guiding teacher becomes pivotal. Whether it's a mentor, a philosophy, or a source of inspiration, identifying someone whose teachings resonate profoundly can be a beacon on your journey. Applying their principles to your life becomes a compass, guiding you toward a future filled with the richness of newfound potential and opportunities.

The Growth Mindset for Healing

The key to unlocking the transformative power of healing lies in embracing a growth mindset. Renowned psychologist Carol S. Dweck's work illuminates the concept that our abilities and intelligence can be developed with dedication and perseverance. In the realm of healing from trauma, adopting a growth mindset means viewing challenges as opportunities for learning and development rather than insurmountable obstacles (Puff, 2021).

For instance, instead of seeing a relapse into old patterns as a failure, a growth mindset perceives it as an invitation to reassess and refine the healing approach. This mindset cultivates resilience, fosters a positive relationship with oneself, and propels individuals forward on their journey to recovery. The true magic lies in recognizing that healing is an ongoing process, and every step, regardless of its size, contributes to the flourishing garden of personal growth.

Cultivating Joy in the Everyday

In pursuing healing, it's time to rethink where joy resides. Contrary to the common belief that it's exclusive to grand occasions, the real magic unfolds in everyday moments. By reframing our frame of reference, we untangle joy from milestones and embrace the small pleasures strewn along our daily path (Barron, 2023). Let's discover some simple yet powerful ways to enjoy your life.

1. **Joy in the Small Moments:** Challenge the notion that joy is reserved for significant milestones and learn to celebrate the beauty scattered throughout your daily routines.
2. **Savoring Life's Pleasures:** Allow your heart, mind, and body to fully acknowledge the pleasure present in each moment by embracing a slower pace.
3. **Embracing the Neutral Middle:** Find joy in simplicity by appreciating the contentment of moments that are not marred by problems, fostering gratitude for the subtle beauty in the world.
4. **Cultivating Joy in Every Step:** Incorporate mindfulness into your daily life to transform each small instance into a source of joy, painting your healing journey with vibrant positivity.

Reinforcing the Message of Hope

In the intricate tapestry of healing, reinforcing the message of hope becomes a guiding light.

1. **Set and Achieve Goals:** Craft a roadmap to your aspirations, setting achievable goals that pave the way for a journey illuminated by personal victories.
2. **Stick with Positive People:** Surround yourself with those who nourish your spirit, creating a vibrant ecosystem of positivity that fortifies your resilience.
3. **Focus on the Present:** Amid life's complexities, find solace in the present moment, where hope blossoms in the gentle embrace of mindfulness.
4. **Be Self-Reflective and Confident:** Harness the power of self-reflection and unwavering confidence, two anchors that steady the ship on the hopeful seas of transformation.
5. **Keep a Positive Outlook:** Gaze into the horizon with a positive outlook and witness the unfolding chapters of your journey through the lens of boundless possibility.

Encouraging Continuous Self-Love and Self-Growth

Embarking on the journey of continuous self-love and growth involves cultivating a flourishing inner garden. Here are key techniques to tend to the blossoming oasis within:

1. **Practice Mindfulness:** Immerse yourself in the richness of each moment, practicing mindfulness as a gentle breeze that nurtures the roots of self-awareness.

2. **Be Honest About Your Weaknesses:** Acknowledge your vulnerabilities as seeds of authenticity, fostering a soil where genuine self-growth can take root.

3. **Speak Sincere Words of Self-Acceptance:** Let the language of self-acceptance flow—a river of sincere words that irrigate the soil of self-love, fostering a climate for growth.

4. **Forgive and Self-Forgive:** Allow forgiveness to be the healing rain that nurtures your inner landscape, fostering an environment where self-growth becomes a natural progression.

5. **Know Your Values:** Illuminate your path with the guiding stars of your values, anchoring the journey of self-love and growth in a foundation of purpose.

6. **Practice Good Self-Care:** Treat yourself with the care of a devoted gardener, ensuring that your well-being becomes the rich soil in which self-love and growth flourish.

7. **Stop Comparing Yourself:** Release the shackles of comparison and let your uniqueness bloom as individual petals in the diverse garden of self-discovery.

8. **Set Boundaries:** Erect boundaries as guardians of your sacred space, creating an environment where self-love and growth can thrive without infringement.

Empowerment Affirmations: Crafting a Symphony of Self-Positivity

In the symphony of self-empowerment, affirmations resonate as powerful melodies, shaping the narrative of our well-being, anxiety relief, overcoming depression, and fostering a positive self-image (Montijo, 2021).

Affirmations for Well-Being

1. "I find joy in everything I do," a melody that infuses mundane tasks with the vibrant hues of happiness.
2. "My body is healthy, and my mind is at peace," a rhythmic assurance that echoes the harmony of holistic well-being.
3. "Opportunities come my way easily and effortlessly," a cadence inviting the dance of abundance into life's grand ballroom.
4. "I enjoy loving and respectful relationships," a harmonic affirmation fostering connections that sing with mutual care.
5. "I am confident, and I am enough," a resounding anthem declaring self-worth and inner strength.

Affirmations for Anxiety Relief

1. "I am dealing with this the best way I can, and that is enough," a soothing mantra serenading the acceptance of one's efforts.
2. "I let go, and I'm at peace," a tranquil refrain that calms the anxious storms within.
3. "I am safe, I am strong, I am well," a powerful chorus embodying a fortress of security and resilience.
4. "I see the positive in every situation," a harmonious perspective shift orchestrating calm amid the chaos.
5. "I'm ready and capable to handle everything," a bold declaration of readiness, tuning the mind to face challenges.

Affirmations for Depression

1. "I am loved and supported by the Universe," a cosmic ballad affirming the vast network of love surrounding me.
2. "I forgive myself," a gentle melody ushering in the healing winds of self-compassion.
3. "Today I take another step toward positive change," a motivational rhythm propelling the journey out of darkness.
4. "I am Love, and I am Light. All is well," a mantra illuminating the internal landscape with the radiance of positivity.

5. "I deserve love and happiness," a heartfelt chorus acknowledging one's inherent worthiness.

Affirmations for Self-Image

1. "I am enough," a foundational chord affirming completeness in the present moment.
2. "I love myself yesterday, today, and tomorrow," a timeless melody echoing self-love across the continuum of time.
3. "I am worthy of love," a soul-stirring refrain recognizing the inherent value within.
4. "Productivity does not define my value," a liberating anthem detaching self-worth from external achievements.
5. "I am at peace in my body, my mind, and my life," a serene symphony embracing tranquility in every aspect of being.

As we conclude the chapter, we stand on the precipice of transformation, having navigated the intricate landscape of healing and self-discovery. The journey embarked upon is not just a collection of pages turned but a testament to the resilience that resides within.

MAKE A DIFFERENCE WITH YOUR REVIEW

Unlock the Power of Generosity

"In the aftermath of narcissistic abuse, every act of kindness we extend to others plants a seed of healing in both their heart and ours, blossoming into a shared sanctuary of recovery and hope."

Did you know that when we do nice things for others without expecting anything back, it can make us feel really worthwhile? It's like when you share your favorite snack with a friend, and it makes you both happy. That's the magic of being generous!

So, I've got a special question for you...

Would you be willing to help out a friend you haven't met yet, even if they might not be able to say thank you?

Think about someone who's feeling really mixed up and hurt inside because of the way someone else has treated them. Maybe they're feeling a lot like you did before. They're looking for a little bit of light in a pretty dark place, but they're not sure where to find it.

I want to help everyone feel better and find their way out of that dark place. Everything I do is about helping more and more people. But I need your help to reach as many people as we can.

That's where you come in! Believe it or not, what you think

about this book can really help. When you tell others how this book helped you, it's like you're holding out a flashlight in the dark for them to see by.

So, on behalf of a friend out there who's still looking for that light, could you take a minute to share how this book helped you?

It doesn't cost anything but a little bit of your time, and it could really make a big difference for someone else. Your words might help...

...another kid feel less alone.
...another family start to heal.
...another heart to find courage.
...another person to take that first step.
...another story to have a happy beginning.

To spread some kindness and hope into someone's world, all you need to do is share your thoughts about this book. It's super easy and quick! Just scan the QR code below to leave your review:

Scan here!

If the idea of helping someone out there makes you smile, then you're exactly the kind of friend we're looking for. Welcome to the circle of kindness!

I'm so excited to be on this journey with you. The tips and ideas we're going to explore together are going to help you so much.

Thank you from the very bottom of my heart. Now, let's jump back into our adventure of healing and growing stronger together.

Your friend and guide,

K. C. Mallette

P.S. - Remember, sharing a little bit of kindness can make a big difference. If this book has helped you, and you think it could help someone else, why not pass it along?

CONCLUSION

In my end is my beginning.

T. S. ELIOT, THE FOUR QUARTETS

Navigating the terrain of healing is far from a straightforward path. It demands patience, urging us to embrace the discomfort and traverse the intense, unsettling emotions that accompany profound loss or pain. Suppressing these feelings may only delay the journey to a better place, reinforcing the notion that the only way to the other side is through the depths of our experiences.

In this expedition toward healing, relationships emerge as invaluable companions. Love and support from those dear to us act as a healing tonic for the body, mind, and soul, boosting our spirits and providing fresh perspectives. As we delve into the unique process of healing, the importance of perspective becomes apparent. It's a paradox that life-altering events, such as illness, can be seen as unexpected gifts, jolting us into viewing life differently. Discovering life's profound significance amid challenges becomes an unparalleled gift.

Healing, as depicted in the family stories shared in *How We Heal*, is a bespoke journey. The heart of the matter lies in discovering what holds meaning and purpose for each individual. The avenues to healing are diverse, whether through art, music, writing, nature, prayer, meditation, gratitude, or the embrace of loved ones. Allowing oneself to love and be loved emerges as a cornerstone in this intricate process, a pivotal aspect that contributes profoundly to the healing tapestry.

As we conclude this book and embrace the dawn of a renewed life, let's carry forward the wisdom gathered. Each person's journey is a unique narrative, a testament to resilience and self-discovery. Together, we've woven a collective tapestry of triumph over the shadows of narcissistic abuse. Success stories are not mere tales but guiding lights, illuminating the path for those still finding their way. In sharing our stories, we foster a community of thrivers where collective strength becomes an unstoppable force.

Standing at the threshold of renewal, let's not forget the transformative power within us. In the spirit of unity, resilience, and perpetual growth, let our stories be chapters in a collective narrative of triumph over adversity. Your voice holds immense power, your journey is an inspiration, and together, we illuminate the path toward thriving. As we part ways, I extend a heartfelt invitation to share reflections, join our community, and, if these pages offered solace and guidance, consider leaving a review—a beacon for someone else seeking the light on their healing journey.

RESOURCES

Ackerman, C. E. (2023). *21 Mindfulness Exercises & Activities For Adults (+ PDF)*. PositivePsychology.com. https://positivepsychology.com/mindfulness-exercises-techniques-activities/

Arabi, S. (2017). Why Survivors of Malignant Narcissists Don't Get The Justice They Deserve. *HuffPost*. https://www.huffpost.com/entry/why-survivors-of-malignant-narcissists-dont-get-the_b_59691504e4b06a2c8edb462e

Arzt, N. (2021). *What is communal narcissism?* Choosing Therapy. https://www.choosingtherapy.com/communal-narcissism/

Barron, K. (2023). 3 simple ways to cultivate joy every day. Mindful. https://www.mindful.org/3-simple-ways-to-cultivate-joy-every-day/

Better Help Editorial Team. (2023). *The Importance of Setting Boundaries: 10 benefits for you and your relationships*. Better

Help. https://www.betterhelp.com/advice/general/the-impor tance-of-setting-boundaries-10-benefits-for-you-and-your-rela tionships/

Blackstock, J. (2023). *The Relationship between Intuition and Trauma - Taproot Therapy Collective.* Taproot Therapy Collective. https://gettherapybirmingham.com/the-relationship-between-intuition-and-trauma/

Bremner, J. D. (2006). *Traumatic stress: effects on the brain.* Dialogues in Clinical Neuroscience, *8*(4), 445–461. https://doi.org/10.31887/dcns.2006.8.4/jbremner

Burgemeester, A. (2022). What Does a Narcissist Want in a Rela tionship? - The Narcissistic Life. *The Narcissistic Life.* https://thenarcissisticlife.com/what-does-a-narcissist-want-in-a-relation ship/

Burgemeester, A. (2023). *13 signs the narcissist is preparing to discard you.* The Narcissistic Life. https://thenarcissisticlife.com/13-signs-the-narcissist-is-preparing-to-discard-you/

Casabianca, S. S. (2022). *7 signs Someone doesn't respect your boundaries and what to do.* Psych Central. https://psychcentral.com/relationships/signs-boundary-violations

Cherry, K. (2023). *11 Signs of Low Self-Esteem.* Verywell Mind. https://www.verywellmind.com/signs-of-low-self-esteem-5185978

Cherry, K. (2023). *What is Cognitive Behavioral therapy (CBT)?* Verywell Mind. https://www.verywellmind.com/what-is-cogni tive-behavior-therapy-2795747

Cheyette, B. (2021). Why it's important to celebrate small successes. Psychology Today. https://www.psychologytoday. com/us/blog/1-2-3-adhd/202111/why-its-important-celebrate-small-successes

Chowdhury, M.R. (2023). *Emotional regulation: 6 Key skills to Regulate Emotions*. PositivePsychology.com. https://positivepsy chology.com/emotion-regulation/

Chughtai, F. (2023). *Overt narcissist: 8 signs, causes and how to deal with them*. Narcissist Hunter. https://narcissisthunters.com/ what-is-overt-narcissist/

Conversations With A Clinician. https://www.convoswithaclini cian.com/post/how-to-communicate-your-boundaries-effectively-to-others

Cuncic, A., MA. (2023). *Effects of narcissistic abuse*. Verywell Mind. https://www.verywellmind.com/effects-of-narcissistic-abuse-5208164

Dalla-Camina, M. (2021). How to set effective boundaries. *Psychology Today*. https://www.psychologytoday.com/us/blog/ real-women/202112/how-set-effective-boundaries

Damascan, I. (2021). It's not impostor syndrome, it's all the years of internalized bullying and criticism! *Medium*. https:// medium.com/rewire-institute/its-not-impostor-syndrome-it-s-all-the-years-of-internalized-bullying-and-criticism-11c1f74e5287

Davis, E. (2021). The 7 Things I learned about Loving Again After Abuse. Goalcast. https://www.goalcast.com/7-things-i-learned-about-loving-again-after-abuse/

Dawson, A. (2023). *Narcissistic abuse and self-esteem.* Counselling Directory. https://www.counselling-directory.org.uk/memberarticles/narcissistic-abuse-and-self-esteem

Dixon, J. A. (2022). *7 tips for setting realistic aspirations about your dreams and goals in life.* Youth Employment UK. https://www.youthemployment.org.uk/tips-for-setting-realistic-aspirations-goals/

Dong, M., Anderl, C., & Kaleigh A. Decker and Charles G. Lord. (2023). *How narcissism relates to social media.* SPSP. https://spsp.org/news-center/character-context-blog/how-narcissism-relates-social-media

Drescher, A. (2023). *Narcissistic love bombing cycle: Idealize, devalue, discard.* Simply Psychology. https://www.simplypsychology.org/narcissistic-love-bombing-cycle.html

Flamingo, M. (2022). *Financial independence and life planning: the ultimate recipe for happiness.* Money Flamingo - FIRE & Lifestyle Blog. https://www.moneyflamingo.com/financial-independence-and-life-planning/

Fry, A., & Dimitnu, A. (2022). *How To Relieve Stress for Bedtime.* Sleep Foundation. https://www.sleepfoundation.org/sleep-hygiene/how-to-relieve-stress-for-bedtime

Furlan, J. & Schneider, C.M. (2022). How to set boundaries with family — and stick to them. *NPR.* https://www.npr.org/2021/01/25/960423678/how-to-set-boundaries-with-family-and-stick-to-them

Gillis, K. (2023). Learning to trust after an abusive relationship. Psychology Today. https://www.psychologytoday.com/gb/blog/invisible-bruises/202204/learning-to-trust-after-an-abusive-relationship

Grande, D. (2023). *15 tips for setting boundaries with a Narcissist.* https://www.choosingtherapy.com/setting-boundaries-with-a-narcissist/

Greenberg, E. (2021). How Do I Heal from Narcissistic Abuse? *Psychology Today.* https://www.psychologytoday.com/us/blog/understanding-narcissism/201807/how-do-i-heal-narcissistic-abuse

Hall, J. (2016). *Emotional resilience escaping low self-esteem.* The Law Society. https://www.lawsociety.org.uk/topics/blogs/emotional-resilience-escaping-low-self-esteem

Hargitay, M. (2023). 6 steps to support a survivor. Joyful Heart Foundation. https://www.joyfulheartfoundation.org/6-steps-to-support-a-survivor

Hart, W., Breeden, C. J., Kinrade, C., & Lambert, J. (2022). Antagonism and narcissism as a conditional relationship: The role of social-engagement traits. *Personality and Individual Differences, 190,* 2-10. https://doi.org/10.1016/j.paid.2022.111534

Herman, K. (2021). Six Self-Care Tips on Overcoming Abuse-Related Trauma. https://nami.org/Blogs/NAMI-Blog/January-2021/Six-Self-Care-Tips-on-Overcoming-Abuse-Related-Trauma

Hurtado, A. (2023). Victim Advocacy: Guide to supporting survivors of Domestic Violence | Maryville Online. Maryville University Online. https://online.maryville.edu/blog/victim-advocacy-guide-domestic-violence/

Johnson, B. (2019). Psychotherapy: Understanding group therapy. https://www.apa.org. https://www.apa.org/topics/psychotherapy/group-therapy

Kidd, K. (2022, December 29). *6 tips to keep your brain healthy*. Mayo Clinic Health System. https://www.mayoclinichealthsystem.org/hometown-health/speaking-of-health/5-tips-to-keep-your-brain-healthy

Kippert, A. (2023). *Stages of recovery after trauma*. Domestic-Shelters.org.   https://www.domesticshelters.org/articles/after-abuse/stages-of-recovery-after-trauma

Klinzing, A. (2023). *Navigating boundary ruptures: Restoring balance and building resistance*. Cleansing Vibes. https://cleansingvibes.org/navigating-boundary-ruptures-restoring-balance-and-building-resistance/

Koprowski, B. (2023). *How empaths and people with narcissistic personality disorder may interact*. https://www.medicalnewstoday.com/articles/empath-and-narcissist

Krill, W. E. (2023). A survival checklist for the victim of a narcissist. *PairedLife*. https://pairedlife.com/problems/An-NPD-Survivor-Checklist

Lancer, D. (2020). How childhood trauma makes us vulnerable to abuse. *Psychology Today*. https://www.psychologytoday.com/

us/blog/toxic-relationships/201905/how-childhood-trauma-makes-us-vulnerable-abuse

Lazarus, A. (2018). *Multimodal Therapy: A Primer*. Dr. Ofer Zur. https://drzur.com/multimodal-therapy/

Lindberg., S. (2020). *Benefits and options for therapy*. Healthline. https://www.healthline.com/health/benefits-of-therapy

Lopez, K.J. (2018). Abuse survivor has a message for other victims: You are not alone. Aleteia — Catholic Spirituality, Lifestyle, World News, and Culture. https://aleteia.org/2018/09/13/abuse-survivor-has-a-message-for-other-victims-you-are-not-alone/

Mason, A. (2023). Signs of Emotional trauma in Adults: Recognizing and Addressing the symptoms | All Points North. *All Points North*. https://apn.com/resources/signs-of-emotional-trauma-in-adults-recognizing-and-addressing-the-symptoms/

McDowell, A.D. (2022). Self-Trust is the foundation of trusting others. Brainz Magazine. https://www.brainzmagazine.com/post/self-trust-is-the-foundation-of-trusting-others

Melissa, C. (2023). *PTSD Statistics and Facts to know in 2024*. The Recovery Village Drug and Alcohol Rehab. https://www.therecoveryvillage.com/mental-health/ptsd/ptsd-statistics/

MHA (2023). Find support groups. Mental Health America. https://mhanational.org/find-support-groups

Minor, N. (2020). *9 Assertiveness Techniques To Help Reinforce Your Personal Boundaries*. Natasha Minor Counselling &

Psychotherapy. https://natashaminor.com/9-assertiveness-techniques-to-help-reinforce-your-personal-boundaries/

Montijo, S. (2021). How to use positive affirmations for a fulfilling life. Psych Central. https://psychcentral.com/health/what-are-positive-affirmations

Moore, K. (2021). *The difference between walls and boundaries - Blossome*. Blossome. https://www.blossome.support/2021/11/15/the-difference-between-walls-and-*boundaries*/

NCADV (2023). Resources. National Coalition against Domestic Violence. https://ncadv.org/resources

Neal, A. (2021). *Setting boundaries is an act of Self-Respect*. BEST SELF. https://bestselfmedia.com/setting-boundaries-self-respect/

Nichols, L. (2023). 10 Ways Resilience Helps as You Recover from a Narcissistic Relationship - Moving Forward with Hope. *Moving Forward with Hope*. https://www.movingforwardafterabuse.com/resilience-after-narcissist/

Olivine, A. (2023). What to know about support groups. Verywell Health. https://www.verywellhealth.com/support-group-5205220

Pal, P., Hauck, C., Goldstein, E., Bobinet, K., & Bradley, C. (2023). *5 simple mindfulness practices for daily life*. Mindful. https://www.mindful.org/take-a-mindful-moment-5-simple-practices-for-daily-life/

Pedersen, T. (2022). *Dating a narcissist: Common signs and what to do*. Psych Central. https://psychcentral.com/disorders/how-to-know-if-youre-dating-a-narcissist

Perry, E. (2022). *Positive affirmations: 30 affirmation examples to use daily*. Better Up. https://www.betterup.com/blog/positive-affirmations

Puff, R. (2021). The path to personal growth. Psychology Today. https://www.psychologytoday.com/us/blog/meditation-modern-life/202106/the-path-personal-growth

Raypole, C. (2018). *Rational Emotive Behavior Therapy*. Healthline. https://www.healthline.com/health/rational-emotive-behavior-therapy

Raypole, C. (2019). *Malignant narcissism: What it actually means*. Healthline. https://www.healthline.com/health/malignant-narcissism

Raypole, C. (2023). *Covert narcissist: Signs, causes, and how to respond*. Healthline. https://www.healthline.com/health/covert-narcissist

Reid, J. (2023). *The science behind gaining distance from the narcissistic abuser*. Jay Reid Psychotherapy. https://jreidtherapy.com/science-behind-gaining-distance-from-the-narcissistic-abuser/

Relojo-Howell, D. (2022). *5 Ways Narcissistic abuse affects your body and mind*. Psychreg. https://www.psychreg.org/narcissistic-abuse-affects-body-mind/

Remes, O. (2023). *Why are we becoming so narcissistic? here's the science*. The Conversation. https://theconversation.com/why-are-we-becoming-so-narcissistic-heres-the-science-55773

Rice, H. (2017). *Be your own therapist: A beginners guide to self-reflection*. Counselling Directory. https://www.counselling-directory.org.uk/memberarticles/be-your-own-therapist-a-begin ners-guide-to-self-reflection

Robins, A. (2023). *How to reconnect with yourself and live the life you desire*. tonyrobbins.com. https://www.tonyrobbins.com/mind-meaning/3-ways-reconnect/

Schneider, A. (2015). *Idealize, devalue, discard: The dizzying cycle of narcissism*. Good Therapy. https://www.goodtherapy.org/blog/idealize-devalue-discard-the-dizzying-cycle-of-narcissism-0325154

Schoenfeld, T. J., & Cameron, H. A. (2014). Adult neurogenesis and mental illness. *Neuropsychopharmacology*, *40*(1), 113–128. https://doi.org/10.1038/npp.2014.230

Shaw, E. (2023). The narcissist and trust. Overcoming Narcissistic Abuse - Elizabeth Shaw. https://wasitme.blog/2020/10/05/the-narcissist-and-trust/

Simon, G. (2018). Narcissism spectrum. Retrieved from https://www.drgeorgesimon.com/narcissism-spectrum/

Smith, I. (2021). *How Does Trauma Affect the Brain? - And what it means for you*. Whole Wellness Therapy. https://www.wholewellnesstherapy.com/post/trauma-and-the-brain

Sweet, P. (2023). *How gaslighting manipulates reality*. Scientific American. https://www.scientificamerican.com/article/how-gaslighting-manipulates-reality/

Tartakovsky, M. (2014). 3 Unique techniques for navigating a negative inner voice. Psych Central. https://psychcentral.com/blog/3-unique-techniques-for-navigating-a-negative-inner-voice

Taylor, R. B. (2011). *Dialectical behavioral therapy*. WebMD. https://www.webmd.com/mental-health/dialectical-behavioral-therapy

Thibodeaux, W. (2020). Want to know if someone is trustworthy? Look for these 15 signs. Inc.com. https://www.inc.com/wanda-thibodeaux/want-to-know-if-someone-is-trustworthy-look-for-these-15-signs.html

Vater, A., Moritz, S., & Roepke, S. (2018). Does a narcissism epidemic exist in modern western societies? comparing narcissism and self-esteem in East and West Germany. *PLOS ONE, 13*(1), 1–16. https://doi.org/10.1371/journal.pone.0188287

Villines, Z. (2023). *What is gray rocking?* https://www.medicalnewstoday.com/articles/grey-rock

Walker, B., & Salt, D. (2023). *The science of resilience*. Resilience Org. https://www.resilience.org/stories/2018-11-27/the-science-of-resilience/

Waller, S. (2018). *8 Ways Narcissists Destroy Your Confidence And Self-Image*. Change Your Thoughts. https://www.stevenaitchison.co.uk/8-ways-narcissists-destroy-confidence-self-image/

Whalen-Harris, R. (2023). *The Importance of Surrounding Yourself with Positivity*. OneEighty. https://www.one-eighty.org/news/the-importance-of-surrounding-yourself-with-positivity/

Wright, S.A. (2021). *How to identify and overcome trauma triggers*. Psych Central. https://psychcentral.com/health/trauma-triggers

Zoppi, L. (2023). *Trauma bonding explained*. Medical News Today. https://www.medicalnewstoday.com/articles/trauma-bonding